C

2 BOOKS in 1

How to Grow Cannabis Indoors

&

DIY Cannabis Extracts

By Scott McDougall

Main Table Of Contents

How To Grow
Cannabis

A Beginner's Guide to Safely & Effectively
Growing Cannabis Indoors

By Scott McDougall

Table Of Contents

Introduction

There comes a moment when a certain spark ignites, and a person decides to venture into the exciting realm of indoor cannabis growing.

Fans of the plant choose to cultivate their own for a great number of reasons.

The benefits include:
- Saving time and money.
- Remaining safe and discrete.
- Access to a consistent supply.
- And, perhaps most importantly, being able to control the variety and quality of the yield.

Growing a garden of cannabis indoors allows you to closely observe its development, without having to deal with the usual array of outdoor pests, nosy neighbors, or harsh weather conditions.

Once you have an ideal system in place, an indoor grow is a very predictable way to grow excellent quality weed. If you do it right, you will not need to look anywhere else to stock up.

Believe it or not, growing your own cannabis can be fairly simple — once you have the materials and know-how to get things underway. Keep in mind, seeds know exactly how and when to sprout, and plants know how and when to bud without any outside influence on our part.

Cannabis is not really meant to be grown as a houseplant. However, a few considerations and modifications go a long way in helping the naturally-grown cannabis plant survive in a highly-controlled indoor space.

The ultimate objective of an indoor grow is to recreate those perfect outdoor environmental conditions within the walls of your home, apartment, shed etc.

With moderate intervention and attention to detail, you can find yourself enjoying a homegrown cannabis in little more than 4 months from the time you tuck in your very first seed.

Since you are reading this book, it is likely that the spark that I mentioned before is already alight in you. You are curious and eager, excited and maybe even a little bit nervous.

There is no need to be anxious about getting started, though. An exploration of the process and all that you can expect to experience as a first-time grower can be found herein. An indoor grow takes a little bit of farming, a tad bit of chemistry, a whole lot of discovery, and yields immeasurable reward.

Sound good?

Well, then — let us get started!

Chapter 1:

Preparation, Part I

Choosing Location

Getting your very first grow up and running can be very exciting. Keep that feeling! You are about to embark on a journey that will surprise you, teach you a lot, and lead you to a having a new skill that can serve you for a lifetime.

But let's not get the cart before the horse, as they say. It is deceptively easy to imagine that you can just jump right in with both feet and figure it out as you go. However, as we all know, haste makes waste — and that is certainly the case with cannabis cultivation.

Without a complete and organized plan, you are likely to find yourself devoting more time and energy to getting out of pitfalls than enjoying the process. And, more importantly, the quality of your buds will take a huge hit, that could otherwise be easily prevented.

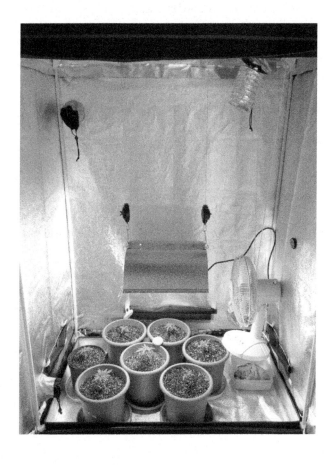

Deciding on your ideal indoor location is a wise place to begin your planning. It is not as simple as it may appear. But do not worry — in the following chapters, we will go   through the most important things you need to consider. As we go through the different criteria, you should check off the pros and cons of each room you are considering.

You owe it to yourself to be methodical about your grow from the very start. It is a sorry day when you realize you have failed your plants by trying to cut corners, and now your plants are failing you in return.

Make sure to put in the effort from the get-go. By being organized and purposeful about the choices you make, you will definitely reap the rewards.

So, what do you need to consider when choosing the best location for your indoor crop?

The following are seven primary factors that will make or break the quantity and quality of your yield.

1. Concealment

Like fine jewelry or a stack of cash, you do not want your valuables to be out in the open for anyone to take a gander at. Although it should be legal for you to grow cannabis where you are, you do not want the whole world to be aware of what you are doing.

Even the hassle of explaining yourself to neighbors or proving your legitimacy to the cops are headaches worth avoiding. Also, a room full of fresh cannabis can be very attractive to thieves. All things considered, make sure you pick somewhere discreet to grow your plants.

2. The Exhaust System

One of the primary difficulties for many indoor farmers is in dealing with the pungent fragrance of a maturing plant. A carbon-filtered exhaust system is the main way most growers ensure that the hounds don't come a sniffin'.

Also, a successful grow depends largely upon the regulation of air temperature and circulation among your plants, as well as in and out of the room itself. The role of an exhaust system is invaluable in allowing fresh air to replace hot, humid, and pungent air once things really get going.

You will want ventilation to suck the moist and warm air out near the top, and cool dry air to be able to enter from the bottom. There are many creative and effective ways to do this. Just be sure you make the exhaust system part of the plan when you decide where to set up your grow. We will discuss the details on how to do this in chapter 2.

3. Area

How much square footage will it take to produce the yield you are going for? This is an important question to keep in mind when considering the footprint of your location.

Additionally, the height must be able to accommodate pots, plant growth, lights, fans, and the spaces in between that are needed to tend to everything and allow for that all-important air circulation.

When in doubt, give yourself a little more room than you think you will need. When it comes to inaccurate measurements, it is much better to have a bit of extra space than too little of it.

4. Sound & Smell

As mentioned, you want your plants to be both out of sight and out of mind from curious onlookers or passers-by. Consider the various means of blocking the sound of humming and whirring appliances, as well as the delicious and heady, totally recognizable, scent of maturing buds.

Carbon filters and sound-insulating foam boards are just two of many techniques you can use to deal with these red flags. If left unchecked, they will potentially draw unnecessary attention to your operation, no matter the size.

5. Transporting Supplies and Yield

Wherever you choose to grow your indoor garden, you will need to first get the parts and pieces in place to set things up. And again, later, once there is significantly more biomass, your crop will be harvested, trimmed and the remains will need to be discreetly removed from the grow space into a place to dry and cure.

If you have your own vehicle and a garage, you may have the ideal location set up right there, attached to your home (or unattached as the case may be). Either way, make sure you plan for it.

6. Running Electricity

In regards to cannabis growing, running electricity provides a unique challenge. Not every room in your house is likely able to handle the high-voltage appliances which an abundant grow requires.

A small setup should be fine to have in your house, using the voltage available for the typical home owner's appliances. However, you want to think about how much that constant draw on electricity will reflect a jump in energy costs for the next 4 months or so.

7. Damages

Finally, it is worth your while to weigh the effects of heat and humidity on your grow space. A cannabis grow tent can minimize these dangers since they are designed specifically to address each variable we have mentioned.

Still, if you decide that a tent is not your style, you should know that there will be certain phases and areas of your grow that may be affected by heat, moisture, and intense light energy.

Even so, every room has some potentially good qualities along with possible drawbacks. Weigh your options realistically, plan accordingly, and you will be well on your way to a smooth operation.

Choosing Lights

If we were to grow our cannabis outdoors, the sun would provide us with all the light we needed. For indoor operations, however, we must creatively utilize alternative sources of energy to power the growth of our plants and plump up our buds.

Cannabis just loves huge amounts of light, and its abundance definitely has a large effect on the quality of the final harvest. The successful indoor grower knows that attention to the quality and methods used for lighting are invaluable to the healthy development of great grass.

When it comes down to it, there are three basic types of lights for you to choose from:

1.   Fluorescent
2.   High-intensity discharge
3.   and the increasingly-popular and readily-available LED

Any of these types of lamps, along with their corresponding housings, can be found at your local home store, or in a specialty retail center that caters to the indoor medical marijuana grower or recreational hobbyist.

When you are starting out, consider a minimum wattage to be 250 per square meter. It is then realistic to shoot for 2-3 times that strength if possible. The more light you supply, the larger, denser, buds you will end up with.

The best practices in indoor cannabis growing also call for keeping the plants as close to the light source as possible, so that the intensity of the light that reaches the leaves and buds can be maximized.

We as growers attempt to optimize light intensity and

work to get our plants right up into that energy. However, it is imperative that we make sure that the plant does not grow so close to a hot lamp that it will become damaged by the heat. Using the back of your hand, you can sense pretty well how the plant would feel at whichever range you test.

Through special suppliers of indoor growing items, you can find "air-cooled" lights that have a glass enclosure over the bulb for extra protection. Forced air also moves over them, which keeps the plants safe even as they grow taller and start reaching towards the lights.

Fluorescent Grow Lights

Fluorescents are a popular choice among home growers because they work really well for indoor gardening — without using a whole lot of electricity. They run cooler, emit a really nice spectrum of light for growing cannabis, and can be used in relatively tiny spaces.

A fluorescent bulb is the very best choice during the

vegetative stage, due to the particular blue color range that they emit. That being said, when it comes to the last stage of growth (when your buds are giving it their all to plump up and pack in all the goodness you are going for) if you are able to fit in a bigger, stronger light, you will end up harvesting significantly-better yields per watt by using an HID or LED grow light, instead of that T5 fluorescent that was good enough during the vegetative stage.

High Intensity Discharge Grow Lights

HID grow lights are significantly more efficient than fluorescent lights, but they have a tendency to get very hot. This increase in the heat requires protection for the surroundings, as well as a careful eye to ensure the plants are never burned.

They should be used along with an air exhaust system to help maintain appropriate temperatures and humidity in the grow area. HIDs are very easy to use once they're set up. If your main goal is to get the highest yields possible, then HIDs can be a great way to go from the start, as long as you take the necessary safety precautions.

LED Grow Lights

LED grow lights can often be found hanging above many indoor cannabis gardens, as they are a very popular choice. These lights are beneficial in that they do not become nearly as hot as other lamps.

You can often find LEDs equipped with built-in cooling features that nearly eliminate the complications and added cost of using high power exhaust fans and ventilation. However, this naturally makes them more expensive.

LED light has a superior ability to penetrate the leaves beyond the uppermost canopy and into the cellular structure of the plant. This results in higher absorption of the energy needed to feed the plant and grow the buds.

Overall, using LED grow lights will require much less adjustment and handling. They will not need to be moved in the same way that fluorescents do. You can simply hang an LED light over your plants and get your grow on.

Choosing Pots

What should you consider when choosing the perfect container for growing your cannabis? Well, the pot is certainly an important source of vigor for your plant; not in itself, but what it holds within its walls.

The sole purpose of the container you opt for is to provide the very best possible environment to nurture the heart of your cannabis: the always-feeding and active roots that support the growth of the plant above.

The pot needs to properly contain and retain all that allows the roots to have adequate moisture and oxygen at all times. It must also allow proper access to nutrients and have a balanced pH.

There are many types of containers for growing cannabis that can be found at local garden centers or online stores. If you are just starting out, you will be safe picking the standard pot-and-saucer option. This simply refers to any container with a hole at the bottom to allow for drainage, along with a dish-type, catch-basin saucer beneath — to catch the run-off water.

What may be most important to consider about your pot choice is not the material it is made of or its physical design, but rather its size or capacity. The final size of your plant will be determined by the health and size of the root mass within the pot you provide. Larger plants obviously require more volume for underground growth. Smaller plants will grow best in a smaller container that can support an immature root system.

In general, aim for 2 gallons of pot volume per 12

inches of desired plant height. This is not a hard-and-fast rule, but more of a guideline that will help you gauge what to aim for. If in doubt, choose a larger pot. No matter what you opt for, be certain that there is adequate drainage, so that the roots are neither drowned nor rot inside the pot because of too much water.

Choosing Growing Medium

One of the freedoms that comes with cultivating cannabis indoors is the ability to pick from any variety of media in which to grow.

What you fill your pot with before growing cannabis is one of the most influential parts of the entire journey. Your growing medium has the important job of protecting the very life source of your plants — their roots.

Healthy roots require constant moisture, oxygen for faster growth, nutrients to feed the plant, and a balanced pH to make sure they are absorbed.

Rockwool

The most common growing media used for weed in a pot have both pros and cons. Rockwool is one such option. It is a mineral fiber, or metal oxide, created using extreme heat and air pressure. It is said to be made similarly to the spun fibers of cotton candy.

It holds a great deal of water, but is without nutrients and can be harmful to the environment. It is used to great effect in seed-starting and in hydroponic operations. However, it needs to be thoroughly rinsed prior to use, in order to wash out any loose irritants and broken fibers.

Soil

The word soil is a loose term for a type of medium that may be composed of any number of elements including sand, compost, manure or peat moss. Soil is, of course, a growing medium that can easily be found at any garden center.

It is abundant, and typically available with specific nutrient mixes added, which will feed the plant without any extra effort of your own for a period of time. However, the plant will eventually take in all of the nutrients, so you will need to supplement in some way. With that being said, soil will usually result in the best-tasting and smelling herb for most people.

Soil naturally keeps pH at a constant level, but can be an expensive option depending on the size of your grow. Once your grow is complete, it is advisable to discard the used soil and replace it entirely, rather than just supplementing with additional fertilizers. Note that soil from your garden should be avoided, because of the potential for bringing in pathogens, pests, and pollutants.

Compost

Another alternative is to use compost as your growing medium. Compost is made of organic materials such as manure, yard waste, and plant matter that has broken down, been acted upon by microorganisms, and has become soil through decomposition or worm composting. Composted, organic soil results in what many cannabis aficionados believe to be a particularly good taste and smell.

It is considered as the very best potting medium of all. This is because it has all of the nutrients needed to sustain the entire grow, has a texture that retains water, yet allows for drainage, and maintains a constant pH, just like regular soil does.

Some people choose to enhance their compost medium with a bit of perlite (more on that shortly) to prevent the compost from becoming compacted. The very best compost is worm compost, which you can make yourself at home, even indoors, and use as an enhancement to whichever medium you opt for.

When growing hydroponic cannabis indoors, most people prefer using rockwool or a number of mediums mixed together. For this book, however, we will focus on growing in a non-hydroponic set up.

The last option is to create a soilless mixture of perlite, vermiculite, and other such materials. If you choose one of these options, you will need to boost them with added nutrients, since, by themselves, they offer no nourishment to your plant. The benefit of this method lies in the fact that, without nutrients, it creates an environment that is very unlikely to harbor pests.

Let us now go through each of these soilless options.

Perlite

First off, we have perlite — a material made of volcanic glass. This glass has been expanded through a heating process, forming it into granules. It is good for growing cannabis because it has a neutral pH, retains water due to how porous it is, and holds a good amount of oxygen. It is particularly light-weight, which makes it a good choice for huge volume containers.

On the downside, perlite is very dusty — meaning it can easily clog the small filters and pumps needed to efficiently care for an indoor grow. In addition, it does not have the stability to support an entire plant by itself. Perlite is generally used in combination with other media to create an optimal mix.

Vermiculite

Vermiculite is a natural mineral made primarily of clay and mica. Like perlite, vermiculite is expanded under high heat. It is used for its ability to retain a good amount of water and is very light.

Like perlite, it is inadequate alone to withstand the weight of an entire plant. It, too, needs to be used in combination with other growing media to provide a balanced potting mixture.

Clay Pellets

Expanded clay pellets are the third of our soilless components that are treated with a high heat, to cause them to expand like Rice Crispies. You may see these referenced as L.E.C.A. which stands for Lightweight Expanded Clay Aggregate. These porous balls of clay have become one of the most popular options among experienced growers. Like perlite, these little balls are neutral in pH.

They are also sterile and able to be re-used. They provide the benefit of having the weight and structure needed for supporting roots of a fully-grown cannabis plant. Plus, they are excellent for providing drainage and aeration.

When clay pellets are used as a medium, the nutrient-rich water is absorbed and retained until it is used by the roots. There is one negative aspect of clay pellets, though: you need to thoroughly wash them before use, due to the amount of dust they create and hold from being factory made.

Coco Coir

Coco coir is derived from coconut husk fiber. It is beneficial in that it breaks down very slowly, making it easily reusable. It has been created as a replacement for peat, which can be environmentally destructive to harvest.

Like all of the other high-performing potting media, coco coir provides water retention, drainage, and aeration. You can find it in many forms, such as bricks, croutons, or mats.

Your Best Choice As A First-Time Grower

When you first try your hand at growing cannabis indoors, it's recommended to purchase an already-balanced medium available at a store. They come with a higher price-tag, but eliminate the question of how to create a mix that will retain water, allow excess to drain off, provide nutrients, and give enough oxygen to the root mass. Basically, it saves you a lot of time.

Once you become more adept at maintaining the

needs of your plants, and have confidence about tackling the soil, you can take the next step up — creating your own medium.

An advanced grower saves money by mixing bulk materials to create the ideal mix for his or her specific strain of cannabis. A homemade planting medium is usually created using a common core of ingredients that include bases such as peat moss or coco coir.

To further fill up and round out the base soil, cannabis growers include additional items that also serve to create air pockets and better water drainage. The best options for helping to support the moisture content of your roots include lava rocks, wood chips, perlite and vermiculite.

Other growing methods can be used without the need of soil, such as hydroponics. Hydroponics can be done indoors, but it has a tendency to become quite complex. For that reason, we will not cover all the details of it in this book.

Choosing Nutrients and Fertilizer

Growing cannabis indoors for the first time can be intimidating and confusing if you feel like you need to master chemistry to get it right. Using premeasured fertilizers takes the difficulty out of it. These can be easily purchased online or in most garden centers.

The first two steps in selecting and using a quality feed are:

1. Understanding the purpose of the various nutrients.

2. Recognizing the signs of deficiencies that will call for supplementation.

You will find that most fertilizers show a series of 3 numbers. They represent Nitrogen (N), Phosphorus (P), and Potassium (K).

Nitrogen

Nitrogen is utilized throughout all aspects of cannabis' growth. It is a building block component used in plant cells, enzymes, chlorophyll and protein production. As you probably learned in school, chlorophyll is what converts light energy into the carbohydrates the plant uses for growth.

In most cases, a nitrogen deficiency in your cannabis is easily identifiable by stunted growth in combination with yellowed leaves, or a purplish tint on the underside of leaves and along the stems.

Essentially, you only need to know which levels of nitrogen to offer at which stage of growth. Do not worry, though; after the seedling stage, which is taken care of by the soil, there are only two growing stages for cannabis — the vegetative stage and the flowering stage.

Use a high-nitrogen formula during the first stage of life, when the plant develops its green matter, stems, and leaves. Then, once your plants are lush and fully ready to support bud growth, switch to a low-nitrogen formula to guide them into the flowering stage.

Phosphorus

Phosphorus plays a key role in the transferring and storing of energy within your plant. It works in tandem with nitrogen to ensure your plant is able to use what energy it has available. A deficiency of phosphorus would be identifiable in a plant with stunted growth along with blotchy spotted leaves, or those that turn dark and curl under.

Generally speaking, phosphorus levels during the vegetative state should be half of the nitrogen. After entering the flowering stage, the need for nitrogen lessens, and so phosphorus levels will increase in percentage.

These different levels of balance are usually included

in premade nutrient mixes from garden stores, most often with labels mentioning "vegetative" and "blooming" (sometimes called "flowering").

Potassium

The element of potassium is necessary for a number of critical processes within the cannabis plant. For example, it helps build cell walls and aids in the ability to flower and take up water.

It is also influential in helping the plant to resist the stresses of environmental factors, diseases, and pests. A potassium-deficient cannabis may show leaves that have rust-colored spots, stems that become weak and brittle, leaf edges that look burned, and tips that curl upward.

Achieving & Maintaining Balance

The appropriate amounts of nutrients per feeding are just as important as the right balance between the parts. Too much fertilizer can burn your plants' leaves, and also deposits components that leave the buds with an unpleasant taste. Nutrient deficiencies, on the other hand, will yield weak and underdeveloped plants.

You may be surprised to find that deficiencies are often directly related to the pH of the water. The pH level is what determines how well the roots are actually able to absorb the nutrients in the soil.

You can easily check the pH each time you water by using a digital pH pen. I highly recommend purchasing one to eliminate any stressful guesswork. If your reading shows that you need to enhance your soil, a fast and efficient way is to mix sand and compost into the potting medium. The sand provides great drainage, and the compost provides rich nutrients and moisture retention to the soil.

So, what kind of nutrients should you opt for — organic or chemical? Ultimately, it really comes down to personal choice. Organic nutrients are most natural and will create the best-tasting, most fragrant, and smoothest-smoking herb.

On the other hand, chemical nutrients will do a more

efficient job of boosting essential nutrients, as well as potentially increasing the potency of the flower. These chemicals also come to the plant in a very easily-absorbable form, which may cause faster growth.

Because plants are living, growing, and changing organisms, they require different amounts and elements found in food and water as they develop. They need fuel to maintain their functions, to flower, and to thrive. Without nutrients, a plant cannot be healthy. You can try to raise a cannabis plant without serving its nutrient needs. However, even if the plant survives, it will be short, weak, and result in a very poor yield.

On the flipside, you do not want to overdo it, either. As a general rule of thumb, only add nutrients to every other watering. If you are not sure about the nutrient doses, it is best to reduce them by half or one third. 9 times out of 10, a plant with just a little added nutrition will yield better buds than an overfertilized one.

Chapter 2:

Preparation, Part II

Grow Tents

Growing cannabis indoors will require one of two things: a closet or room within your house, or the use of a so-called grow tent. Grow tents allow you to create an indoor environment that permits you to easily specify, adjust, and manage the conditions you want for growing — wherever you want and at any time.

Grow tents offer a number of benefits that lend themselves particularly well to first-time growers. Even though grow tents can seem complicated, in most cases, the positives outweigh the negatives. In this section, we will look at how they can work for or against your particular needs.

First off, grow tents provide an entirely-closed space that integrates air purification. With this, the strong odors trapped inside the tent can be filtered as they are drawn out, and thus become undetectable from the outside (remember, discretion is key when growing cannabis, even if it is legal). Not only is the air inside of a tent filtered, but it is circulated and vented out as well. This allows fresh air to bring CO_2 to your plants without complications.

Another benefit to the tent being a closed environment is that it eliminates the possibility of an infestation of insects that may hinder your grow. The outlay cost of a grow tent is relatively inexpensive.

Plus, they are very energy efficient. They are lined with a reflective material which ensures that 100% of the light emitted can be used, since it travels all around the room.

Furthermore, the materials are fire and water safe, easy to clean, durable, and impermeable — which means they make it easy to maintain consistent temperatures and humidity.

Grow tents are an excellent opportunity to ensure success even when there are many variables to consider. They work well for most people, but also come with some disadvantages, primarily due to their size. A tent should only be large enough for the plants and the equipment you are using. This means any major maintenance requires you to take the plants out of the tent to tend to them.

Also, once you start cultivating a larger number of plants, you will come to outgrow the tents. You will need much more space, equipment, and access so that you can water and fertilize, prune and harvest your cannabis properly.

Air Circulation & Ventilation

Among all the factors that go into growing the cannabis plant, it is the quantity of air-flow that most affects the strength of its structure.

Creating a constant flow of air circulation is the most common way of providing a kind of stress that the plants will respond to by strengthening their main stem. This can be achieved by using an oscillating fan.

Most growers have found that incorporating an oscillating fan has other benefits as well. Imitating a natural breeze is an important factor in helping to recreate an outdoor experience for the indoor plants. The movement of air within a grow area helps reduce hotspots under lights and within dense canopies of maturing plants.

Proper ventilation also forces out the excess humidity that tends to accumulate inside a closed room. Humidity is what fosters the growth of mold and other fungal diseases that will damage your crop. That makes it our responsibility as growers to make sure we bring in and circulate cool clean, oxygen-rich air to our plants, and that we vent out what is old, hot, and moist.

Warm air rises, so it makes sense to install an exhaust fan near the ceiling of your enclosure. The intake can be placed near the floor, where fresh oxygen can get right up close to the roots. Once again, remember that the air surrounding your plants will take on a strong odor. It is wise to use a carbon filter to remove odors from this air before extracting it. This way, you do not let everyone in the neighborhood know what is going on behind your closed doors.

The plans for extracting or venting out saturated air, as well as drawing in and circulating fresh air, need to be part of the initial planning stage — before you set up your room or tent.

Using CO2

Cannabis plants absorb carbon dioxide and release oxygen through their leaves, via the process of transpiration. It is very much like our breath, but in reverse.

We humans breathe in oxygen-rich air and breathe out carbon dioxide. Plants, on the other hand, take in this carbon dioxide and release oxygen. Cannabis, and other plants, need CO2 to turn light energy into energy for growth, which is done through photosynthesis.

Usually, there is more than enough CO2 in the fresh air that is vented into the space where your plants grow, and they can use up their light energy without assistance. However, if there is more light energy offered than they can absorb, providing additional CO_2 to the growing environment allows the cannabis plant to increase their uptake. This significant adjustment cranks up that photosynthesis and gets things growing really quickly.

However, this method only applies if you are already doing everything you can to boost the growth of your chosen strain. Injecting additional CO_2 would not be effective if you only are using fluorescent lamps, for example. But, when it does make sense to use, supplementing with CO_2 can yield up to 20% larger plants at a much faster rate of growth.

Carbon dioxide also allows for the air temperature to be kept safely at higher levels than usual without damaging the plants. It is common for indoor farmers to put significant effort into keeping the temperature low enough to maintain the needs of their plants.

Allowing the temperature to safely rise a few degrees lowers the amount of work you will need to do to maintain the otherwise safer cool temperatures.

Keep in mind that using high levels of CO_2 may require extra efforts in making your grow area completely airtight, in order to maintain the desired levels. However, shutting your grow room this tight also provides the added benefits of energy efficiency and the isolation of sounds and smells.

Keep in mind that it can be expensive to add a great volume of carbon dioxide. When you are first getting started, this method requires equipment that takes additional time and money to set up properly.

Some home growers use a do-it-yourself approach to providing carbon dioxide, by setting up a fermentation of yeast in sugared water. This fermentation reaction releases carbon dioxide into the air and can be a much cheaper alternative.

Getting your levels balanced require the use of a CO_2 meter. This will help you know how to adjust each of the variables that create the air that surrounds your plants. It takes a bit of controlling to ensure you are adding carbon dioxide safely and effectively. If you use too much CO_2 relative to the amount of light, your plants may be damaged.

So, be sure to gradually add more light as you increase the carbon dioxide. If you are producing plenty of high-quality light in your garden, levels of 1000 to 1500 ppm (parts per million) is considered optimal for boosting cannabis growth.

A quick health warning: keep in mind that CO_2 levels of 5000 ppm may cause headaches and nausea, while 10 000 ppm and up can be toxic to humans and other animals. So, get a reliable CO_2 meter, keep an eye on the levels, and stay safe!

Chapter 3:

Seeds, Part I

Cannabis Strains

Scientists continue to discover, and gain a deeper understanding of, the unique qualities of popular varieties of weed, even as new ones crop up.

While the average consumer becomes more educated on what is available, and how to use it medicinally, we see two types, or strains, emerge as the clear favorites. These have a more or less equal following, in addition to a number of blended hybrids of the two that continue to be highly sought after.

The two primary varieties of cannabis are named Indica and Sativa.

Indica

Canabis Indica plants grow to be squat and bushy. They typically max out in height under six feet tall and are characterized by wide-fingered, deep, green leaves. Their origins reach back to the ancient times of the Middle East.

The feeling you get from enjoying a quality Indica strain is relaxed and social. The strongest varieties numb the body and lead to deep relaxation that is great for meditation. As a medication, Indica strains are used to treat seizures, migraines, chronic pain, sleep disorders, as well as relieving stress. This marijuana variety tends to be widely available since it is presumed to be easier to grow, has a high quantity yield of tight, big buds, and are quicker to grow than the Sativa strain. Indicas are often identified as having a pungent or sweet aroma and particularly-strong flavors.

Sativa

Cannabis Sativa plants grow much taller than an Indica — reaching nearly 25 feet tall. However, they can be kept under 12 feet with some structured maintenance.

These plants have long, thin, light-green leaves and are what the typical marijuana icon represents. The Sativa strain produces light, fluffy buds which take many more weeks to finish than an Indica.

The feeling you get from a Sativa is usually uplifting and energetic. Compared to Indica, it can be great for daytime use.

Sativa can be used to alleviate bodily pain and clinical depression, as well as mental and behavioral disorders in general. Sativa also tends to stimulate hunger, which has been proven useful for patients suffering from the effects of chemotherapy or anorexia.

Hybrid

Hybrid strains offer individuals the characteristics people like best from both strains. Expert marijuana scientists isolate the genetic components of uniquely selected Sativa and Indica strains they most wish to combine. Then, they join them together to create super strains that manifest the chosen aspects of both parents.

Strains labeled as hybrids will always be predominantly Sativa or Indica, and have the characteristic flavors, looks, and effects to match the dominant features the plant was hybridized for.

Medical and recreational cannabis use now reach far beyond the boundaries of the Earth's tropical climates. For many, however, availability to flower is limited, so growing indoors is the only option that makes sense.

Luckily, it has never been easier to have great success growing in the privacy of our own homes. It all begins with superb-quality seeds. Get yours from a supplier who is trustworthy and has a track record of developing great strains.

The Best Strains for Indoor Growing

Online shopping has made it simple to access nearly any variety of cannabis you could think of. But, with so many strains available, which are most suitable to grow indoors? To choose what is best for you, first, decide what you are looking for in a strain.

Consider the size of the plant, the length of time the flowering period is expected to last, and amount of yield you count on harvesting. Of course, there is also the taste and effect to consider. Some strains should be expected to be more in need of an experienced growers' keen eye, instincts, and patience to get that plant to reach its full potential.

When it comes down to it, picking your ideal strain for indoor growing will be a very subjective choice. There are however five strains that consistently rate highly among home growers.

These most legendary strains include White Widow, Power Plant, Northern Light, Cheese, and Sweet Bubble. Each of these strains are available to the home grower and can be bought as seeds.

Where To Buy Seeds

Cannabis seeds can be found for sale online through a bunch of different seed banks, which are mostly located in areas where the laws on selling are more relaxed. Some of the most sought-after strains are available online from the following companies:

- Greenhouse
- Dutch Passion
- Kulu
- and Royal Queen Seeds

Be wary when purchasing from outside of the United States; attempting to have seeds sent by mail into what is a federally illegal cannabis country can get them confiscated by customs or border protection.

In legal states, seeds are readily available for purchase at dispensaries. Seed banks in many states will often ship seeds anywhere in the US with discrete and well-sealed packaging.

Feminized Seeds

Feminized cannabis seeds are those that have been treated in a particular way to make only female plants as offspring (which are the only ones that produce buds). This leads to the creation of plants that are nearly identical to the mother plant.

If you want only budding cannabis, the easiest option is to just buy feminized seeds from a trusted supplier. However, you can also make them quite cheaply yourself, should you choose to do so.

There are several ways to make feminized seeds. The most popular and reliable method is to use colloidal silver to transform the mother plant into a hermaphrodite plant. This will then make seeds that will only produce females.

To create feminized seeds, follow these steps:

1. Buy, or create, colloidal silver.

2. Locate a female cannabis plant and spray the bud sites with colloidal silver daily during the first 3-4

weeks of flowering.

3. Look for swollen pollen sacks that are starting to open up. Carefully remove them from the plant and put them in a plastic bag or container.

4. Let them dry for 3-4 days, and then shake the bag or container to efficiently collect the feminized pollen from the sacks.

5. Pollinate another female cannabis plant that is about 3 weeks into the flowering stage. You can easily do this by using a small brush to distribute the feminized pollen to the bud sites of the new mother plant.

6. Wait about 5-6 weeks for the feminized seeds to fully develop, then harvest them.

7. Use the seeds immediately or store them in a dark and dry place.

Determining Seed Quality

Generally speaking, you can assume that all darkly-colored seeds are viable for growing. You can also assume that any pale-green or white seeds will not germinate. They are usually completely dried out and have lost their life. On the other hand, most shiny and dark seeds will germinate easily when given good conditions.

When I first began looking closely at cannabis seeds for propagation, I thought that the only good ones were those that were very hard and dark. I figured that if I squeezed them and they stayed intact, they were likely able to grow.

Little did I know that way more factors go into the viability of a seed then its skin tone and the hardness of the coat. I later realized that a seed about to sprout is naturally quite delicate, which completely trashes the aforementioned theory.

The best way to find out if a seed is good for growing is to simply try to germinate it. However, be careful to only test what you are willing to grow, or else you may find yourself having to throw away what could have been a great plant.

When seeking out seeds, it is essential that you find reputable retailers to get the very best quality product. The long-term benefits are definitely worth the initial time and money investment.

If you want to avoid retail and rather source seeds from a local grower, a friend, or collect them yourself, there are several qualities you should look for in order to get a great yield.

First off, the seeds must be fully mature before being harvested. They should look plump, never brittle nor dull, and should look almost shiny, or at the very least smooth.

They need to be properly stored in a cool, dark place so that they do not mold or become infected by any pathogen. If you do see mold, mites or tiny holes, the seed has been compromised, and should be discarded or at least not relied upon for the best quality yield.

The most important factor in determining the quality

of the seeds is one that cannot be seen by the naked eye — genetics. For this reason, experienced breeders who have put the time into developing particular strains for their best characteristics will be the most trustworthy source of seeds.

Even a perfect-looking seed may grow a less-than-great plant if its parents were weak. On the flip side, an average-looking seed may have been bred over generations to produce easy-to-grow, potent buds — and given the chance, it will do so.

As long as you provide the right conditions for germination to take place, even what may appear to be a weak seed can grow into a hardy specimen. Bottomline: If you have the opportunity, check out the family tree of your cannabis.

A seed's shelf life usually extends up to 16 months, unless frozen for long-term future use. Just keep them cool, dry, and ideally out of sunlight, to preserve their viability as best as possible.

Seed Pests

Pests that can completely mess up your cannabis include:

- Aphids
- Fungus gnats
- Thrips
- Green flies
- Black flies
- Mosaic virus
- Spider mites
- Caterpillars
- Inchworms
- Whiteflies
- White powdery mildew
- Stem rot

These pests primarily survive on the leaf matter, roots and juices of the plant itself rather than the seeds.

Seeds are more likely to be damaged and rendered lifeless from extreme conditions, such as high heat and low humidity, which would dehydrate the seed.

A seed can also be irreparably damaged if there is too much moisture and not enough oxygen for the it to germinate and continue to take in nutrients.

Chapter 4:

Seeds, Part II

Germination

Cannabis germination is what we call the process of getting your seeds to sprout. We know that a seed has germinated when a little white tendril emerges from it and begins to grow towards the earth. That little tendril is the plant's very first root, known as a "taproot".

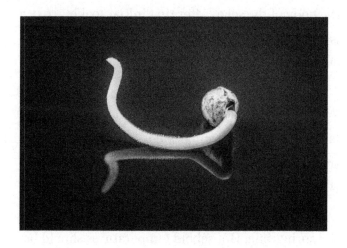

Cannabis seeds are tough little things. They do not take much special treatment to be willing to open up and grow that very first tendril. You do not need to allow them to freeze or scratch their surface to encourage their growth.

Water and warmth are enough to set the process into motion. However, you are most likely to have successful germination if you are able to offer a perfect balance of moisture, oxygen, and temperature.

If you want to get a jump on germination, you can soak hard seeds for a day to soften the exterior coat. This will allow more water to penetrate through to the body of the seed. After that initial soaking, oxygen is equally important, so be sure to allow the seed a chance to breathe.

With those two factors taken into consideration, your last way to aid in germination is to make sure the seeds are put in a draft-free place to grow, where temperatures will remain comfortably warm. Outside, naturally-occurring seeds germinate during the springtime. Household temperatures should be just right for mimicking a perfect range that is neither too hot nor cold.

There are lots of ways to get your seeds off to a strong start into the seedling stage. These are all tried and true methods of at long last starting your plants. For each of the following techniques, it is extremely important that you are gentle with the fragile taproot.

Always plant with the root pointing downward, so that no extra energy needs to be spent by the seedling trying to reorient itself. Remember that this is only the beginning — you will later need to transplant your seedling into a larger container that will more appropriately accommodate the growing root mass and vegetation.

Rockwool And Plugs

Using Rockwool cubes and seedling plugs are two very popular options which are used primarily for hydroponic growing. These manmade options have some advantages to the first-time indoor grower, such as the ability to retain a great deal of water.

Rockwool cubes also hold enough oxygen so that overwatering need never be a concern. Plugs come in a variety of sizes and can even come wrapped in plastic, so that spills are more or less eliminated.

As mentioned earlier, however, Rockwool is in no way an environmentally-friendly option, since it does not decompose. It can, however, break down and be ingested through our lungs.

The dust and fibers of Rockwool are known irritants, so it is advisable to wear gloves and a mask when working with it, so as to protect your skin and airways. Lastly, Rockwool has a particularly high pH, which requires frequent amendment for the health of the roots that need to access nutrients while living within it.

If you choose to use this method, it is simple to begin with germination by seeding directly into a soaked Rockwool. This way, it will stay in the same place until it is ready to be transplanted to its first small container.

Direct planting is another simple option. Using this

method requires only planting the seed pointy side down into the soil within a pot. Just push the seed beneath the surface and use water to make it sink in. Keep the Rockwool moist until you see the first signs of life emerging from the dirt. You should expect to see something in less than a week's time.

Overnight Soak

Soaking overnight is another useful way of getting the seed to germinate fast. To do this properly, place the seed in a cup of room-temperature water for up to 36 hours. The water will be absorbed right through the seed coat, speeding up the process of germination. After the soak, you can plant your seed in any way you wish.

The Paper Towel Method

One way that many growers use to keep a close eye on a bunch of seeds is to use the paper towel method. This is an efficient way to easily begin germination of as many seeds as you like in one go.

The way to get started with this method is to gather a few paper towels and dampen them with clean, fresh water. Between the layers of wet paper towels, you place as many seeds as you would like to get started. Lay the paper towels flat on a paper plate that can also absorb and retain water, so that the towels are less likely to dry out.

To further avoid them drying out, you can place this whole set up on a plate and overturn a second plate to seal off the top. You can watch as your seeds germinate, while easily picking out those that do not. It can take anywhere from hours to days for your seeds to germinate if they are kept at a comfortable room temperature range between 65-75°F.

The Germination Station

A Germination Station uses growing medium within an all-in-one mini greenhouse to allow for better control of temperature and humidity. This is a commercially-available product that has one more element to provide warmth from your seeds' very first days.

A heating mat set below the medium allows everything to remain at an ideal temperature for quick germination. The plastic lid above the newly-planted seeds retains the moisture so that your medium stays evenly wet.

The Germination Station is comprised of a plastic tray full of individual cells for each plant to start its life within its own little space.

You can start dozens of plants in a very small area using this method, and any growing medium can be used to fill the cells. It should be placed in the dark at first, since cannabis seeds prefer it for germination. Then, as the sprouts begin to emerge, the entire tray should be moved out into the sunlight or artificial light, as the case may be.

There, they may continue to grow well-protected until it is time to transplant the seedlings into a larger place, to allow for root development and the next stage of vegetative growth.

Chapter 5:

The Vegetative Stage

Just weeks after you have set your seeds into the growth media of your choice, you will see the first sets of true leaves begin to work their photosynthesis magic. True leaves are those that have the typical fan shape we are so familiar with.

The first leaves that emerge from the seed will not have the toothed edges. Do not let that confuse you, though — these will fall away fairly quickly, once the true leaves have begun to take over the process of photosynthesis.

As these first true leaves absorb the light from above, they will draw energy deep down into the developing root system.

Then, the central stem will become the primary pathway through which nutrients are drawn up into a beautifully-developing, lush, green cannabis plant. This is known as the vegetative state.

During this period of vegetative, or green leafy, growth, your chosen strain of cannabis will create as much foliage as it can by using all of the light, water, and nutrients it can absorb.

It will then transform this into sugars to form the strong supportive structure for the buds it will eventually bear.

At this time of rapid growth, your plant can add an inch or more to its body every single day. On average, you can expect the vegetative stage to last about 4 weeks when starting from seed.

Each individual strain's genetics, plus the growing methods used, will determine more accurately the speed at which your plant will grow and move through the different stages of development.

Making the very most of your controlled environment and the variable factors such as light, air, temperature, and humidity will allow you to boost the results of the vegetative stage.

These weeks are the prime time for you to prepare the plants' root system and fan leaves, to later nourish and support the very best bud development possible for your chosen strain — do not neglect it!

Light

The light cycle that you choose to use during the vegetative stage must remain consistent, and should provide around 18 hours on and 6 hours off. Both light and dark periods contribute to the overall health of your plants.

However, the balance should always be tilted towards more light. You will be secure as long as you do not offer any more than 10 to 12 hours of uninterrupted darkness. This will keep your plants safely maintaining vegetative growth.

Ideally, a full or whiter spectrum of light can be used to most closely mimic what the sun would provide outdoors in the middle of summer. Refer back to the section on artificial light options covered in the first chapter to remind yourself how different bulbs will power your plants' growth.

Air

Just like plants that are raised outside through the summer months, your indoor plants appreciate having a steady breeze of fresh air blowing through their branches. While the plants are young, make sure to keep the velocity of air movement low, so as not to damage your plants or interrupt their growth.

You can increase the air current velocity when you see the stems hardening off and becoming more resistant to the breeze. This artificial wind serves to strengthen the structure of the stems, so that they can later withstand heavier yields of bud. Needless to say, this is highly beneficial.

Temperature

When considering the ideal temperature of your grow room or tent, you can expect that there will be a variation between "lights on" and "lights off" periods of the day. Aim for a balmy 75-85°F while the overhead lights are in the "on" position, and a comfortable 70-75°F while they are "off" — when the plants are in the dark.

One more thing to keep in mind about temperature regulation, is that you do not allow it to rise and fall so drastically that the plant becomes stressed by the changes. At the max, you should allow a swing of no more than 18°F between the "lights on" and "lights off" temperatures.

Humidity

Temperature and humidity go hand-in-hand. The warmer the air, the more water vapor it can hold. As we extract warm air from our grow areas, moisture is also removed. There needs to be a nice balance of air temperature and humidity so that things neither dry out too quickly, nor grow mold.

A wide range of 45 to 75% relative humidity (which can be measured with a cheap, digital humidity meter) will be safe for your plants to grow in. These levels can be maintained pretty easily with proper ventilation, adequate watering, and keeping the temperature within an ideal range.

Since the range is so wide, it may sound like a no-brainer. However, it is vitally important to the health and development of your plants that you get this right — be sure to keep the levels in check.

When the humidity levels are medium to low, your cannabis is better able to absorb water and nutrients given through feedings. The plant will quickly react to the nutrients given, and will demonstrate its health through the color of its leaves. Conversely, if the humidity is too high, the plant will not be able to absorb the nutrient-rich water, and may stop growing until the balance has been restored.

A good rule of thumb is to start your plants off with a high relative humidity of around 70%, before dropping it by 5% each week until you can maintain it at 40%.

Nutrients & Water

During the active weeks of vegetative growth, your plant requires a high concentration of nitrogen to build up as much of that green leafy matter as it can. You will likely deliver this extra nitrogen through the roots, by way of water enriched with nutrients.

You should check your planting medium daily to see how much water is available to the roots. If your soil is dry to the touch, it needs H_2O as quickly as possible. On the other hand, if the soil is completely soaked, you run the risk of drowning the roots and disallowing oxygen.

It is reasonable to expect that your cannabis will want to be watered at least every other day during the vegetative state, due to the heavy drinking and nutrient use. Be careful to neither over nor under water your plant.

Drooping leaves that are wilted are a sign that the plant needs more water. Drooping leaves that are curled under tell you the plant is already at its water limit. If that is the case, you can lay off of watering at least another day or until the leaves have returned to normal.

In general, the vegetative stage is one of marked resilience. It is during this time that pruning, gender identification, and major growth all contribute to laying the foundation for a healthy and useful cannabis plant.

Pruning & Bending

Done well, pruning and bending lead to overall higher yields of valuable plant matter. It takes planning, purpose, and a bit of precision to make sure these tricks of the trade are done right.

Have no fear if the idea of pruning or shaping your plants makes you uncomfortable. Remember that, even when left alone, nature will do a great job on its own to get your plant to produce the buds its genetics prescribe. Pruning will just give nature a nice boost, so that your cannabis produces bigger and more plentiful buds.

Basically, pruning involves clipping off specific parts of the plant to encourage additional and stronger growth wherever you want it. When you cut away a plant's top, or at a place along the stem just above a budding spot, the two new branches will grow where there used to be only one.

Just like that, you can double your potential weed crop. It does take a plant time to recover from being pruned, though, as the cuts create stress that it will need to heal from. Still, if you are patient, you will reap the rewards.

There are many styles of pruning. Each has its own set of risks and rewards to consider. "Topping", as the name implies, is a method that involves removing the main stem near the top of your plant. Done over time, this creates an upside-down cone shape, which allows maximum light energy to reach the bulk of the leaves in the upper canopy.

"Super cropping" is another popular method, which is done by crushing a stem's soft inner structure to stimulate stronger growth and increased potency. This is achieved by forcing a plant to heal and reinforce the pathways that provide water and nutrients to the outer reaches, where the flowers will grow.

Topping and Super cropping are considered to be high-stress means of pushing a plant toward increased vigor, because of the physical damage that it takes to get the plant where you want it. With that in mind, they should be performed with the utmost care and attention to detail.

"Bending", on the other hand, is a safer, low-stress method you can use if you are feeling unsure about your skills. Bending is done by gently tying branches down while they are soft so that they are horizontal.

Bending the main stem over causes side shoots to be fooled into thinking they instead are primary. This results in them growing straight up — plus, they get bushy and eventually bud heavily.

Many growers employ a method that trains the plants to grow somewhat sideways beneath a type of widely-spaced screens, which allows only the buds to grow upright while the stem lays flat.

This technique is called SCROG (which stands for Screen of Green). This keeps as much of the growth as possible equally distant to the lamps, thereby maximizing the coverage and efficiency of your light sources.

Many other methods of both high and low-stress pruning are out there to be tried. Take your time to find one that best suits your style and comfort level.

Following a few tips will keep you and your plants safe as you experiment with pruning:

1. Always use sterilized and sharp tools to prune with, rather than tearing parts away with your hands.

2. Never strip an entire stem of its leaves — they are crucial to photosynthesis.

3. Water your plant just after pruning, to minimize the lasting stress of being cut.

4. Be careful about how you discard your clippings (again, even if its fully legal, evidence of possession is best kept away from prying eyes).

Transplanting

It may seem like transplanting cannabis is a waste of time. Why would you not just plant your seed where you want it to grow from start to finish?

Well, first of all, let me tell you that you can indeed start your seed right where you intend it to stay for the duration of its life. However, that causes other complications that are easily avoided by transplanting a few times throughout your grow.

The truth is that transplanting is recommended for growing cannabis plants, and actually serves to make them grow faster along the way. If you start your weed in a small container, they will grow faster than if you start them in the pot they will eventually grow into. The reason is that the tiny roots can more easily get the right balance of water and oxygen when they are in a container that fits them well.

Still, in time, a small container will no longer be enough to allow for that perfect balance. At that point, unless you move it into a larger one, your plant will become "root-bound". This means that the roots run out of space and begin to grow around the inside wall of the container. If that happens, it cannot effectively take up the water and nutrients it needs to thrive.

To prevent your plants from becoming root-bound, it is essential that transplanting takes place just before the roots reach the edges of their container. Luckily, the fan leaves above give a good indication of the size of the root mass, since they reach out to about a similar diameter.

A basic guideline for timing your transplants can be followed by first starting your seeds in a germination station. Once the roots begin to grow out of the bottom, gently transplant the plug into a solo cup with drain holes punched into the bottom and sides of it. When the leaves reach the edges of the cup, cut the cup away and transplant again into a 1, 2, or 3-gallon pot.

When the plants have doubled in height, transplant them once again to a larger or final container. Keep in mind that your plants are likely to double or triple in size from the start of their flowering stage. Use a container that is large enough not to tip, and which is able to contain the root mass.

One of the best ways to keep your plants from the shock of transplanting is to water them well a day or two before you go through with it. This will hold the growing medium together and help it to slide out of its container.

Before removing the plant from its small holding, have your new pot already prepared for the transplant to be placed in its center. The growing medium should be watered, and the hole should be dug to a size equal to, or greater than, the container your plant has grown out of.

Loosen the root mass from its container by running a knife around the inside edges. Lay your hand flat on the dirt with the main stem between your fingers. Invert the pot if you are unable to lift the plant with your fingers alone. Stabilize the dirt and roots with your opposite hand as you transfer the plant into its new container.

Water the plant in once you have repotted it. Add

more soil if you need to level out the top to cover the roots. Pat it down gently and water again. If you are nice and gentle, your plant will be happy to make this transition, and will not stress at all. You will be rewarded with vigorous growth and stable plants that can withstand being moved without toppling.

Chapter 6:

The Flowering Stage

The flowering stage is what follows the vegetative period of growth. This is when you will start to see and smell the "fruits" of your labor. The flower of the cannabis plant is the bud you will ingest once every part of the process has come to completion.

During the flowering stage, all of the plant's energy goes into creating male or female parts. If you have successfully gotten your female plants to bud, and it has begun to really fill out, you can be sure that they are no longer in danger of being fertilized.

Pre-Flowering

Even before your plants enter into the flowering stage, it is best to be certain about the gender and expected outcome of what you are investing in. Many weeks before the first true flowers even open, a cannabis plant will develop "pre-flowers" at the crux of a leaf and stem. Pre-flowers are an immature, yet accurate, demonstration of a plant's gender.

Male pre-flowers are spade-shaped, and generally show up earlier than their female counterparts. Female pre-flowers are more elongated toward the top and usually have one or two whispy-white pistils that emerge from the tip. You will most often find pre-flowers growing closest to the light source by the 6th week of growth. These will help you determine if a plant will be worth your time, space, and energy to nurture completely into the flowering stage. Occasionally, a random male flower will appear on an otherwise female plant. This is an anomaly that causes no danger to a mature plant. If you see this happening, simply snip off the male flowers — the female buds will continue to develop unhindered.

Lighting

When you are controlling the growth of cannabis indoors, artificially switching the plant from vegetative to the flowering stage is done by changing your light cycle to an even and consistent 12 hours of light, followed by 12 hours of total darkness. It is the dark period, in particular, that signals your plant to start putting its energy into flowering, rather than toward more vegetative growth.

The initial phase of a 12/12 schedule is often referred to as the "flowering stretch". You will understand why when it seems like your plants have suddenly doubled in height. This first part of the flowering stretch phase is between 1-3 weeks long. During this time, your cannabis plant will also develop bud sites.

Getting more light to these areas will mean more bud down the road, so consider training or pruning while the stems are still flexible during the vegetative stage. These two methods are both good ways to increase your harvest. We covered how to effectively manipulate your plants for the most output in Chapter 5.

The next few weeks (4-6) are still considered early in the flowering stage. The female plants are becoming quite showy, with more than a few white tufts of pistils emerging from the jointed part of the stems. At this point, many pistils reach out, seeking fertilization from pollen in the air.

Notice how I only mentioned the female plants. Remember, it is only from a female plant that you will get that treasured bud growth. By this time, male plants will have grown green pollen sacs instead of pistils.

Most growers choose to remove all of these male plants from the grow area, so as to keep their ladies pure and the resulting bud free of seeds. A male plant allowed to develop fully will have mature sacs that open and pollinate the nearby females. This is no good for the home grower who is looking to have high-quality, smokable weed.

In this phase of the flowering stage, some newer growers may fear that the vegetation at the top of the plant is blocking the light from reaching the leaves below. Indeed, a few leaves may begin to yellow or droop a bit. This is nothing to be concerned about, however, as long as it is relatively few leaves being lost and bud growth continues to develop.

The buds of real substance have yet to fill out to their full potential, but should be fattening up by the day. This is an exciting time, as the fragrance of your maturing plants really begins to fill the air!

The last few weeks (6-8) of the flowering stage focuses all of its energy into bud growth alone. For this reason, more of those bottom leaves may yellow, and only the buds are showing significant development.

During this phase, you should be feeding your plants less nitrogen, since it is not the green leaves that need any further growth. Rather, it is phosphorus that is needed in higher quantities than the potassium and nitrogen. This can be easily served up with a mixture of water and wood ash, initially in half doses every 1 to 2 weeks or in a high-quality compost tea on a similar schedule.

Chapter 7:

Harvest

For many newbies, the harvest feels like the exhale after trying to hold your breath in a contest with your buddies in grade school. You think it is time to relax because it is all over. In reality, though, it is not.

The harvest is just the beginning of the final act. The lights are not on yet, and the curtains have not closed. Costly mistakes in the flushing, cutting, and curing of your buds can destroy what otherwise might be Cannabis Cup worthy.

Timing

Your first lesson in this most crucial stage is to recognize when the harvest is going to be. You do not just jump right in and chop everything down. This is a step that will take some time to prepare your ladies for.

The ultimate potency of your nuggets depends on pretty precise timing, slowly weening the nutrients away, and, to an extent, dehydrating the plants. Cultivating too early or too late will rob you of prime-quality resin and THC content.

A few telltale signs will be clear enough for even a novice to recognize that that buds are ripe for picking. The simplest way to know is by checking the condition of the pistils, or long hair-like protrusions that cover the buds.

At their earliest stage, they are white. As the buds mature, the pistils become darker — eventually becoming dark red or brown. Specific strains of marijuana will have their own set of characteristic colors to watch out for.

A microscope will allow a grower to check out the resin glands, also known as the trichomes, of the cannabis plant.

The trichomes are what appears as white crystals to the naked eye. This is where the THC is located. They, too, change color — from clear to creamy, then amber. A harvest should take place before they reach the color of amber, which is when they start losing most of their potency.

Flush

Now, the thing about harvest is that, weeks before you can actually cut, you must prepare the plants so that the buds will be great for smoking. This requires one or more "flushes".

A flush is usually begun two weeks before the harvest by removing all remaining nutrients from the growing medium. This way, the plant uses up what sugars, starches, and other compounds remain in its vegetation for energy. Left inside the plant, these elements will result in awful smokability and a less-than-great taste.

The exact way to flush is to over-irrigate the potting medium, until every bit of nutrients and salt that surrounds the roots is dissolved and washed away. Running an overabundance of water through the medium a couple times, over a few minutes apart, will be sure to clean out what remains from around the roots.

One last flush should be done a day or so before you harvest, followed by a full day without any water at all. This important step allows the cannabis and grow room to begin to dehydrate, so that the plant can produce as much resin as possible in its final hours in dry conditions.

When at last the big day arrives, you will want to work in relative darkness. This is done to maximize the pure flavor of the bud that is left, without being tainted by compounds drawn up from the roots once light begins to signal the initiation of the feeding process.

With loppers or strong clippers, sever the main stem apart from the root ball. Keep larger stems connected to the main stem to create places to hang for drying.

Fan leaves can be snipped away from largest to smallest, until you have only the buds and the most heavily-resonated sugar leaves within the bud remaining.

Chapter 8:

After Harvest

After weeks of tender, loving care, you have successfully harvested, and the buds are in your hands. But wait — you are not quite done yet. You may be jumping out of your skin with anticipation, but it is the final touches that will take your bud from potentially harsh to heavenly.

To ensure the ultimate quality from your freshly-harvested buds, you need to finish them off with a process known as curing. The curing stage begins the very moment you cut down your plants.

Drying

Once your plants have been cut, trimmed, and hung, you must tend to the important drying process that sets the stage for the desired outcome of your controlled cure. Taking the time to allow your buds to dry properly will boost the enjoyment potential of your weed, however you choose to consume it.

The amount of drying time depends on what the relative humidity and temperature are where your weed is hung to begin its curing process. The optimal temperature should remain right around 70°F with a humidity of around 50%. In these conditions, you can expect the initial drying phase to last about 3-7 days.

Speeding up the drying process artificially (by using an oven or microwave, for example), will most likely make your finished product smell and taste terrible.

If you started with primo seeds that you expect to have good genetic qualities, you owe it to yourself to do this right. Do not mess this part up by cheating due to impatience— it is not worth it.

To ensure a nice, slow dry, give your buds enough room around each other so that air can circulate. This allows the moisture to evaporate away and not be absorbed by neighboring buds. Letting the flower dry out protects your weed from the mold and bacterial growth, which can otherwise really mess up your smoke.

Keep an eye on the process at least once daily, to make sure that your precious buds are drying out evenly. You will know when they are just right if the smaller stems crack off, rather than bend, when you test their flexibility.

Curing

Once the initial dry is complete, the curing process can continue for up to 6 months in sealed glass jars, bringing the buds up to their peak potency. The temperature during this period can stay the same as throughout the initial dry — 70°F. Humidity can be a bit higher — around 60-65%.

You will want to open the jars to allow the buds to "breathe" for a minute or two each day, for 2-4 weeks, before closing them back up again. This allows the moisture that remains in the buds to be released, which lets dryer air come in. Over time, this results in an even balance of low moisture. Curing buds for a few more months and opening them to breathe weekly will only continue to improve the quality of your grass.

Over the course of curing your freshly harvested buds, the chlorophyll will break down, which hugely improves the taste and smoothness. Basically, this means you will be less likely to cough or experience a headache from your finished product.

Cured buds are also less likely to come with negative side effects such as paranoia or anxiety. The unique flavors and fragrances of each individual strain will become more prominent as they cure, along with a marked increase in potency.

Packaging & Storing

If you intend to keep any weed for longer than 6 months, it is advisable to package it for long-term storage. Long-term storage is best achieved by using a vacuum-sealed container kept in a cool, dark place other than the freezer. Never freeze your weed — your trichomes will be prone to crystalizing and breaking off, leading to a worse-tasting, less psychoactive weed.

Furthermore, it is absolutely essential that the humidity is kept low at this stage, so that no mold or mildew can grow on your plant matter. For this reason, it is important to try to eliminate great swings in temperature, which, unchecked, could cause condensation to form within the glass jars or bags. When in doubt, opt for too dry rather than too wet.

Regenerating Plants

After months of care, a rewarding harvest, and a trial of patience through the curing process, there is yet another a way to squeeze even more out of your cannabis. It is called regeneration. This is an approach that will allow you to harvest more than one crop from the same cannabis plant.

Of course, you could just cut your plants down and call it a day — hoping to regenerate your beloved plant from the stump. However, it is much more efficient to follow a few steps that will ensure a better result with faster turn-around time.

Proper Cutting

What you should start with is one careful, initial cut. For this, you should aim to clip off the top one-third of the main stem. Hold your clippers horizontally and cut straight through. Your intention here is to create the cleanest and smallest wound possible.

Cutting straight across, rather than on the diagonal, creates a smaller, circular wound as opposed to an oblong one. Make sure that the clippers you are using are sharp and large enough to go smoothly through the main stem, without leaving any jagged or rough edges behind.

Since you will be making more cuts later on, you need to sterilize your tool after use. You can use a solution of 10% bleach to 90% water, or just regular hydrogen peroxide. Allow the blades of your tool to soak for a few minutes. Then, rinse in clean water and dry completely. Now, your clippers should be ready to go into the plant once again.

From the second or middle-third of the plant, you should remove only the bud material, leaving as many of the fan leaves in place as you can. From the bottom or lowest-third of the cannabis plant that you are trying to regenerate, you should clip off the bud tips, but still allow for some of the nuggets to remain on the branches.

You will later find that it is from these points that the newly-regenerated growth will develop. Therefore, the more you leave, the faster you will get significant growth once again.

How To Stabilize It

Now that the plant has been all clipped to pieces, its biology will be quite stressed. You will want to tend to the open wound within 10 minutes of slicing it open. Start doing this by capping the wound. This is like putting a band-aid over a cut, or stitching up a gaping hole.

Doing this will effectively reduce the stress being put on the plant and begin the healing process. You can use some good old duct tape to seal off the main stem's wound.

Remember that the main stem serves as the plant's plumbing. Having been cut, the plumbing will now be leaking until it is capped. Not only does the open vascular system mess up the water flow within the plant, but exposed areas let in air, dirt, and bacteria that can potentially cause illness, weakness, or ultimate failure of the cannabis to survive.

To stop the leaking, tear off two strips of duct tape. Center one piece over the cut and smooth it firmly over to allow it to adhere (you may need to trim the piece so that it fits well).

With the second piece of tape, wrap the stem to stabilize the first piece. Press it firmly onto the stem so that the cut area is no longer exposed at all, and the cap is as close to being air tight as possible. When that is done, you have successfully capped the leak.

Refeeding

You can expect that between the dehydrating process of preparing your pot for harvest, leaking plumbing, and the stresses of being cut, your cannabis plant will be thirsty for water and hungry for nutrients.

Prepare your regenerating plant a drink of lukewarm

water (even the shock of cold water at this point is too much). Mix in a solution of your vegetative nutrient fertilizer to a very mild, quarter strength. Your plant will happily drink in this nutritious water and start to regain its vitality.

Once your plant has entered a stage of abundant growth, you will be able to once more increase the nutrient strength you offer at watering times. From the start, watering heavily will encourage the roots to once again absorb what is given.

Provide enough water so that you observe run-off coming from the drainage holes at the bottom of the container. Remember, cannabis plants do not tolerate sitting in water. It could lead to root rot and deterioration of the plant you are working to revive. With that in mind, tilt the container so that excess water can run out.

Light Cycling

When the previously-mentioned steps have been taken, turn the light cycle back to whatever you consistently used during the first vegetative stage of growth. Alternatively, to really kick-start the regeneration phase, switch to a 24-hour "lights on" schedule for just a little while. As soon as new growth is evident, switch back to the regular vegetative light cycle of your choice, so that the plant gets some rest periods once again.

Within a matter of one to two weeks, you should see signs of new growth along the stems and at the sites where you previously clipped. The very first of this new growth will start from the bottom and move its way up the plant.

Once you are happy with the amount of new vegetative growth, and think there are enough fan leaves to support the photosynthesis needed to feed your plant, you can force your plant into the flowering stage once again.

Just as you did in the first round of growing, switch modes by changing up the nutrient balance you are feeding your plant, as well as adjusting the hours of light and darkness.

Depending upon the strain you started with, you can expect to harvest a second flush in as little as 8 weeks from the time of initial harvest.

Conclusion

Congratulations, you have now gone through all the steps needed to grow your very own cannabis indoors! Before you check under your fingernails to see if, in fact, your thumbs have begun to turn green, keep in mind that many unique challenges may present themselves as you prepare to get your grow underway.

The vast array of choices on the subject need not overwhelm you. Rather, it should give you confidence that there are many directions to turn, if you find that any one way does not jive with your own style of getting things done.

It is my sincere hope that this guide will offer some solid stepping stones that will get you to feel confident about making progress, as you begin to explore the world of indoor cannabis growing.

As you probably know, you are certainly not alone in your endeavor. A dramatic rise in popularity has made growing cannabis indoors a hobby that many people try their hand at. Done well, cultivating indoors can produce great quality grass which should easily beat what you get from most retailers or street dealers.

You can return again and again to this book to use it as a reference guide for the steps and points to consider in your growing adventure. To refresh your memory, let us quickly go over a summary of the most important things we covered in this book.

We began with an in-depth look at the way to prepare yourself for the many months it takes to nurture a crop from seed to flower. We have looked at what to consider when planning for a grow room, as well as the components it takes to make sure it runs smoothly (without alerting the neighbors, thieves or other curious people).

We discovered that with a bit of ingenuity and the proper placement, not only will your weed have adequate light energy, but the proper temperature, humidity, cycles of active photosynthesis and rest as well.

You are now ready to source out the appropriate containers and medium to grow in. We covered all the tools, appliances, supplies, and supports you need, which can be found and purchased online with a simple click of the mouse. Just about anything you can think of can be delivered right to your door where, just inside, your plans may begin to take shape.

It is recommended that, for your very first try at growing, you start by taking it slow and small. Expect to learn a lot as you grow, and possibly plan for a successive grow. Follow your first harvest closely, and identify the factors that will make it easier the second time around.

Use a journal of some sort, combined with photo documentation, to measure the growth, interesting findings, and things that you would keep the same or change the next time you grow.

It is exciting to know that this is just the very beginning. You never know what may come of this, your first foray into indoor cannabis gardening.

Keep educating yourself on the many successful ways people have grown and processed their weed indoors. Share your experiences with other novice gardeners and, most of all, enjoy your harvest — you will most certainly have earned it!

DIY CANNABIS EXTRACTS

A Step-By-Step Guide To Making Oils,
Edibles & Other Great Goodies

By Scott McDougall

Table Of Contents

Introduction

As of late, cannabis has become popularly known to treat a number of ailments and illnesses. The once-shady view of this healing herb has become broadened from "dangerous drug" to "effective medicinal plant." It has been known to treat small ailments, such as arthritis and sore muscles, to larger ones, such as glaucoma and insomnia.

The miracle compound in cannabis, CBD (Cannabidiol), has worked wonders in a number of cancer patients, providing an all-natural method to stifling this global killer.

The sweet, aromatic herb can be ingested in many ways, and with new technology, using cannabis can come in the form of a pill, a vape pen, tinctures, and several other forms. Extracts are a great way to use this miracle plant. Cannabis extracts are oils and other products that have been reduced to create often smokeless, but still effective, medicine. One dose can be a mere drop, which can be hidden in any beverage or favorite dish. Cannabis extracts can still be smoked for those who prefer to do so (the dab is a popular example of one of these extracts).

When professionally made, cannabis extracts will have the same characteristics as the buds from which they were made, giving any user the authentic experience of the uniqueness carried in each strain. However, these products are not by any means cheap, and making them can be dangerous if you do not know what you're doing.

Cannabis is a huge market these days, and the new extraction methods have grown very popular with a large number of users. This has predictably boosted cost, as demand for extracts has skyrocketed.

By using this book as your resource, you should be able to significantly reduce this cost, as well as the safety risks, associated with cannabis extracts. By the end of this book, you will potentially be a manufacturer yourself!

In this book, we lay out every chapter with a brief discussion about the extract, supplies that will be needed, and recommended safety precautions. Then, we add diligent and systematic directions to have you making your very own cannabis extracts in no time!

The first chapter will briefly cover health benefits from using cannabis extracts, as well as providing health risks that can be linked to the plant. The second chapter is all about acquiring plant material from others, which is a dire step in making cannabis extracts.

The third chapter will briefly go into how you can grow cannabis yourself. After you are aware of potential health risks and the many health benefits that cannabis grants, as well as what you will need to get started, you will be sent off into a wonderful journey of knowledge!

After reading this book, you will have learned how to make butane hash oil, Rick Simpson Oil, tinctures, cannabutter, edibles such as cookies and brownies (there are two chapters dedicated to this art), hash, bubble hash, rosin (or dabs) and kief.

Each chapter deeply covers with detail what each extract is, how to use it, and most importantly, how to make it. Are you ready to save colossal amounts of cash and become a craftsman in the herb extract department? Well then, let's get started!

Chapter 1:

Potential Health Benefits

What Makes Cannabis Tick?

The coming of cannabis' introduction in the medical world has many drug manufacturers rattling with fear. This all-natural remedy proses very few symptoms and side-effects when compared to other, more conventional drugs, and is easy to make at home. All you need are resources that come in the forms of knowledge and small gardens.

One such blatant comparison can be clearly seen in comparing formal drugs for pain to cannabis. With a lot of opium-based drugs used for pain, one will go through withdrawals when the drug is no longer needed. This will never happen with cannabis, as it does not develop physical dependency in people (however, a slight mental dependency has been known to occur, depending on the user).

If one takes too many pain pills, they will likely overdose — where a trip to the hospital is inevitable and death is very possible. If one uses too much cannabis, however, they may simply suffer from an empty refrigerator or an unplanned nap or two.

Nonetheless, there are some displeasing side-effects that can come with the use of cannabis, and a few health hazards as well. But the benefits from using cannabis, especially extracts, towers over the potential risks. Let us first explore this magical plant, and briefly go over what makes it a remedy.

Without going into complicated chemistry, we will explain what cannabis is and what gives the plant it's medicinal qualities in a straight forward, easy to understand format. Are you ready?

There are two main chemical compounds that make cannabis a healing plant, and those are THC (Tetrahydrocannabinol) and CBD (Cannabidiol). Both chemical compounds combined have made cannabis a healer for many!

THC: Ease Chronic Pain with a Helpful Strain

THC is definitively the most recognized compound in cannabis. THC is literally the stuff that gets you "feeling good". Researchers have tested THC for pain reducing effects, and results have, with each test, proven extremely competent to ease chronic pain.

In the article, *Medical Marijuana: Clearing Away the Smoke* (2012), researchers Igor Grant, J.

Hampton Atkinson, Ben Gouaux, and Barth Wilsey tested the use of THC up against placebos and codeine (an opiate). Their findings found that THC was great for reducing chronic pain. It worked just as well as codeine, but did not have any of the nasty after effects, such as body-bending withdrawals.

However, THC *did* have some psychoactive effects, but they were usually minor and were never permanent. Other side effects consisted of dry mouth, fatigue, muscle weakness, light headedness and slight palpitations. These effects were largely negligible, and happened in fewer cases of newer users for the most part.

At the end of the day, THC is a great alternative to easing chronic pain overall. THC can be used to treat a number of other ailments as well. It has worked wonders in depression, insomnia, eating disorders and anxiety.

CBD: Cancer Be Dead!

CBD has been more of a recent exploration, and the power of this compound has been found to produce miracles in cancer cases. Unlike THC, CBD does not have any psychoactive effects.

If you take CBD, you will not get the same euphoric feeling that THC provides. However, this chemical compound has become famous for how strong it is towards beating malignant, cancerous cells.

CBD pumps oxygen into the malignant cells, causing the buildup of calcium to stifle the cancer cell's growth. Cancer grows in different stages, and as at it gets older in age, it requires more nutrients to survive. If the cancer cannot get the desired nutrients as it grows, it eventually dies, and thus becomes a non-malignant tumor.

THC & CBD: What A Team!

As cannabis contains both THC and CBD, it has become a heavy sword to brandish against cancer, as these two miracle compounds exclusively attack the dangerous cells. Whether or not this awesome team can *cure* cancer altogether is controversial. Still, it is largely accepted that, at the very least, it can play a part in the battle.

Dennis Hill, a biochemist who claims he beat his stage four cancer with the use of cannabis oil, explains in his article "How Cannabinoids Kill Cancer", how the two team up. THC cuts-off energy going to the cancer cell by disrupting its mitochondria. CBD then makes its appearance and pumps the cell full of calcium. The THC also disrupts the calcium metabolism in the cancer cell.

So, as CBD pumps the cell full of calcium, the cell is unable to get rid of the calcium because of the THC. This results in the cell dying or becoming stagnant. To understand this a little easier, imagine that the THC traps the cancer cell in a bubble, and then the

CBD attacks it. With the news of this combination dealing with cancerous cells so effectively, increasingly large numbers of people are turning to different sources of cannabis to treat their cancer.

Sativa (THC) & Indica (CBD)

Of course, cannabis is also used for recreational purposes, to relax and to take the edge off. It can also be used to soften the tension in arthritis, or it can help you fall asleep when sleep is seldom. And if you have problems with appetite, cannabis will have you eating in no time!

Sativa has a higher THC content, giving one the stimulated, heavy feeling — great for sleeping disorders and eating disorders. Sativa is also used for chronic pain cases, such as serious back injuries and broken bones.

Indica is much more packed with CBD, giving one a lighter mental euphoria, and helping people with anxiety and internal inflammatory issues. Indica can be used in the opposite way for eating, as it has been known to deplete appetite. Therefore, it is also suggested for tackling obesity.

When using these strains for recreational purposes, remember this: Sativa produces a *body high*, while Indica produces a *mental high*. It is easy to remember the two as Sativa being "sleepy-time cannabis" and Indica being "day-time cannabis."

Why Cannabis Extracts?

Cannabis extracts generally prove to be a healthier method of consumption. Smoke is not the best thing for you in the long run, and can promote unhealthy blood flow and problems with breathing. With a number of different extracting methods, however, one can get the same desired cannabis effect by exploring many different routes.

Vapors are fume-free, and prove to be easy on the

lungs, as well as enjoyable and *very* effective. Oils and tinctures can be put on just about anything, and these methods completely stifle the presence of smoke. Other extracts, like cannabutter, can be spread on a piece of toast, or can be added to a cake recipe.

Some extracts *do* contain smoke, but the as they are reductions of the cannabis plant, a meager amount of smoke is produced, as no burning vegetation is involved. Extracts like these are any kinds of hash, kief and the very popular rosin. Although these extracts are usually smoked, they produce much less fumes, resulting in a healthier cannabis experience.

If you are using cannabis to treat breathing-related ailments, such as COPD (Chronic obstructive pulmonary disease), where cannabis acts as an anti-inflammatory, it is direly stressed that smoking cannabis, even vapors, is not a good idea.

The same goes if you are treating cancer in the lungs. This is where extracts, such as the oils, butters, and tinctures really come into play. However, before you can start making these wonderful products, acquiring the necessary materials must be considered. The first, and most important, being the plant material.

Chapter 2:

Acquiring Plant Material, Part I: Outside Sources

Thus far, we have established what cannabis extracts are, and how they can benefit users. Now, we will elaborate on one of the most important aspect of making cannabis extracts, this being acquiring the plant material. There are two different ways to go about this, so we will split this facet of cannabis extract production into two chapters. This first chapter will cover cannabis laws and how you can acquire plant material from three main outside sources. These three sources are medical dispensaries, retailers, and cannabis farmers.

Now, I know you would like to start making your cannabis extracts post haste. However, it is of vital importance that you are aware of cannabis laws. These will depend on the State or Country you live in.

And, if the State in which you reside does not advocate the use of cannabis, through either medicinal or recreational use, then you should not attempt to make any of these cannabis extracts at this time. The last thing we want is for you getting in trouble with the law!

What follows is a quick rundown of the laws

pertaining to cannabis in the USA. If you are from another country, please make sure to research your local laws and regulations.

Laws: Medical Cannabis

Cannabis has offered its many healing qualities to those who prefer it over other sources of treatment for illnesses and ailments. However, there are some guidelines and rules that you should be aware of if you plan to use medical cannabis.

If you find yourself in different States, the medical marijuana laws may vary, but they still hold the same basic rules:

- If you are granted the permission by a physician to use medical marijuana, you can use cannabis in the confinements of your home.

- Using cannabis legally is correlative with using any prescription drug; you cannot drive while using cannabis, and use of cannabis in public is restricted.

As a medicinal cannabis user, you have access to a number of dispensaries, better known to many as the "Cannabis Clubs". If you are a caretaker of someone who uses medical cannabis, then you are legally allowed to handle the herb.

However, you are not allowed to use it yourself. As a medical cannabis patient, you are also able to grow cannabis, and can do so collectively. Depending on the State's regulations, growing cannabis is usually allowed between 4-12 plants. In terms of having buds, one can usually have 1-8 ounces.

Even though cannabis may be permitted in your state for medical purposes, the medical cannabis laws still have holes in them. Federally, cannabis is NOT legal, so the federal government can still prosecute you if you grow cannabis.

However, there is somewhat of an unwritten rule with the federal government, and if you pose no threat to society (i.e. growing HUGE amounts of cannabis with the intent to sell) then the federal government will most likely not bother you. Therefore, it is recommended in medical states to grow no more than 8-12 plants per person, so legal problems will not arise.

In States that have legalized medical cannabis, people have been granted the privilege to grow collectively. This means that, if you and a friend have your legal documents, you can both grow medical cannabis together, doubling the amount of plants.

Again, this can be risky business, and one should act warily when growing large amounts of cannabis, as the federal government has really taken a liking to busting large crop owners — even if their intent is for the sole purpose of personal use. It is recommended to not exceed 100 plants when growing in collective groups.

Here are the States and territories that allow the legal use of medical cannabis as of this writing:

1. Alaska
2. Arizona
3. Arkansas
4. California
5. Colorado
6. Connecticut
7. Delaware
8. Florida
9. Hawaii
10. Illinois
11. Main
12. Maryland
13. Massachusetts
14. Michigan
15. Minnesota
16. Montana
17. Nevada
18. New Hampshire
19. New Jersey
20. New York
21. North Dakota
22. Ohio

23. Oregon

24. Pennsylvania

25. Rhode Island

26. Vermont

27. Washington

28. Washington D.C.

If you are living in any of these States, then you have access to medical cannabis, but remember to remain diligent and careful, for federal regulations still strongly stand by their position for zero-tolerance.

Laws: Recreational Purposes

As the wonders of cannabis are becoming more recognized and accepted in society, many States have begun to legalize the use of cannabis for recreational purposes as well. The easiest way to understand these laws is to compare them to the existing alcohol laws.

In States that have legalized cannabis for recreational use, cannabis products are offered at local stores, just like alcohol. One cannot consume cannabis in public and cannot drive while under the influence, just like alcohol. One can create their own and sell at their wish to other users, just like alcohol. You must be 21 to use cannabis, just like alcohol.

Nearly every aspect of recreational cannabis laws mirror alcohol laws. Nonetheless, in States that have just recently legalized the use of cannabis for recreational use, there are still some problems and loose ends to tie up.

Recently legalized in California, cannabis enthusiasts still cannot *buy* cannabis, unless they purchase the herb from a grower, or the buds are bestowed to them from someone who has a medical card.

The biggest loose end thus far is how law enforcement will measure and determine the intake of cannabis in respect to operating a vehicle. In most States that have already legalized for recreational purposes, there is zero tolerance for cannabis use combined with driving.

Here are the States that have legalized cannabis for recreational purposes.

1. Washington (state)
2. Oregon
3. California
4. Nevada
5. Colorado
6. Massachusetts
7. Maine

As clearly displayed by this list, legalizing medical cannabis for recreational purposes is still very far from being nationally accepted.

Obtaining Plant Material

As previously mentioned, cannabis can be obtained either at medical dispensaries, stores (only in cases where recreational use has been legalized and put into effect for a long period), or from cannabis farmers.

In the following section, we will elaborate on some tips and suggestions on how to obtain plant material from each of these sources.

Medical Dispensaries and Retailers

Depending on what you require in your extract, making extracts from flowers can be very costly if you plan to obtain plant material from a medical dispensary, or a retailer. However, medical dispensaries and convenient stores offer good deals on trimmings, which is a mixture of leaves and flowers left over from harvest. This is also a suitable ingredient for extracts, and produces decent results for a fair price.

Buying the actual flowers and producing your extracts can be costly, but will leave you with a better result. If you are trying to make a stronger cannabis extract that has a significant presence of the strain's character, then you are better off just buying the extract at a medical dispensary or retailer; it is more cost effective.

Farmers

Having a friend or a friend of a friend who is a farmer is your best bet to obtaining plant material from an outside source. When farmers harvest, they usually have copious amounts of trimmings or little flowers, known as "budlets". Another good reason to find a farmer is that they usually sell their cannabis for much less than the clubs and retailers. By finding a farmer, you can cut out the middle man and start making cannabis extracts in no time!

Although the three methods mentioned here are fast and convenient ways to obtain plant material for cannabis extracts, they will be a little more expensive — especially if you wish to make higher grade products. There is a way to avoid this, but it takes some dedication and work. However, with dedication and work, you will have more than enough plant material to use.

If you wish to produce large amounts of flowers for a specialized extract, or if you just want to create large amounts of *mid-grade* extracts, then growing your own cannabis plants is by far the most efficient way to obtain raw material.

Chapter 3:

Obtaining Plant Material

Part II: Growing Cannabis

In the previous chapter, we explained how to obtain plant material from outside sources. Although you are provided with flowers and leaves when going through outside sources, it can be excruciatingly costly. Yes, going through an outside source to obtain plant material is much quicker, and proves to be more convenient, but the quality of your extracts will be far from optimal in comparison to growing your own plant material. It takes time and a lot of work, as well as dedication, but the harvest is completely worth it.

We also learned in the last chapter that growing cannabis is legal in certain States and territories; as some require medical use and others have completely legalized the herb for recreational purposes.

Let us remind ourselves that growing cannabis outside these designated States and territories is illegal, and can end in disaster. OK, now that we have that settled, let us cover the basics for growing a most delectable cannabis.

Where Does One Obtain Seeds, or Clones?

Seeds and clones are not hard to find at all. One can find seeds in any medical dispensary, stores that specialize in producing seeds, or from a farmer. Also, you might just find some seeds in your buds. But not all seeds are usable, as when growing cannabis buds, you are looking for a *female* plant. With seeds, it can take weeks before you know if the plant is a male or female.

Male plants, which display little seed pods around stem conjunctions, yield hemp with no THC, and have significantly lower traces of CBD than their counterparts. Female plants, which produce small hairs around stem conjunctions, are the ones you want, as they yield ample buds. Seeds are very cheap, but can be a gamble.

Using clones is more of a sure deal. If you purchase or make a clone yourself, then it is, without a doubt, a female. Clones can be purchased at the same establishments and outlets listed earlier, but they are costlier, depending on the age of the plant. Also, you can clone female plants easily yourself if you have an existing female already. This is simply done by clipping a branch off your plant and putting it in soil, as it will proceed to grow roots of its own.

When doing this, always use sharp pruners or scissors that have been sterilized, and make sure to cut the branch at a 45-degree angle right below new growth that has grown 5-8 inches. Now that we have our plants, let's grow some cannabis!

Outdoor Cannabis

This is the most basic way to grow cannabis, and is highly recommended to try before exploring indoor grow operations. Only veteran growers should do indoor grow operations, as many more variables present many more difficulties. There are various ways to grow cannabis outside, but since this is not the focus of this book, we will merely cover the basics here.

Firstly, you need to be aware of your region. Cannabis thrives in weather temperatures between 55 and 86 degrees Fahrenheit (12 - 30 degrees Celsius). Also, cannabis loves a mellow climate, as storms and turbulent winds can damage her majesty.

Nonetheless, cannabis has been called "weed" for a reason, as it can grow nearly anywhere, and will produce buds if you follow the seasonal guidelines: Start at the end of Spring, and harvest in the beginning of Fall. This depends on how you start, as seeds require more time than clones do.

Secondly, finding the right spot to grow your cannabis is dire. Again, this will depend on where you live, as a healthy plant requires 5-6 hours of *direct* sunlight. If the conditions are warmer, grow your plant in a location that gets early light, so as not to fry your cannabis.

For colder environments, make sure that your cannabis is provided light that comes later in the day, for a warmer and happier plant. Also, keep in mind security issues, as sticky fingers and rolling eyes usually find their way to cannabis gardens sooner or later. Keep your plants safe!

Thirdly, you will want to focus on soil. There are many different soil cocktails that are efficient for cannabis growth, but the basic and easiest type of soil to use is silty soil. It allows for great aeration, and effectively holds warmth for the roots. You can find this soil at the bottom of lakebeds and old rivers, and it is packed with nutrients.

Fourthly, you need to consider fertilizer. New growers should buy specialized fertilizers that are specifically produced for cannabis cultivation. If you do not want to have to worry about mending the soil, then it is recommended to use super soil (organic pre-fertilized soil). This is a more expensive option, but works miracles in your garden.

Fifthly, comes the water. Make sure to water your plant accordingly, as an adult, flowering female can require up to ten-gallons of water every day! Also, make sure the water is clean, and does not contain chemicals such as chlorine; tap water should always be tested beforehand. Keep her hydrated, and she will yield the best crop for your cannabis-extract needs.

Lastly, protect your plants from bugs. Once again, there are many ways of protecting your plants from pestering insects, but the most natural way is to fight fire with fire!

Go to your local gardening store and purchase a box of lady bugs or praying mantises. These helpful soldiers will not eat your cannabis, but will instead eat the other tiny bugs that *will* eat up your precious plants.

A little tip to know when harvesting is to pay close attention to the little white hairs on your buds. When about half of them turn an orange-brown, you will know that it is time to harvest.

Indoor Cannabis

Growing cannabis indoor is a more complicated science, and the various methods easily cross over from simple procedures to eloquent displays of art. The elaboration of this science has produced pages and pages of techniques, formulas, and equipment.

It is recommended that you find a good source that specializes in this area. However, we will quickly go through the basic knowledge you will need to successfully grow cannabis inside your home, to see if it may be an option for you.

Supplies Needed

- A HPS (Hight Pressure Sodium) light.
- A fan.
- A grow tent (or you may create your own confinement).
- Fertilizer (the same as in out-door operations will suffice).
- A timer (this will prove extremely handy).

After you set up your indoor grow room, you can begin. First, germinate your seeds. They require only soil and water to do this. Once they pop up is when you will need to start feeding them light.

Here is where the timer comes in handy. Hook up your HPS light to your timer, and set the timer for 18 hours on, and 6 hours off. Your cannabis will require this light cycle for up to 4 weeks in time, as the vegetation stage commences. Remember, cannabis is a very thirsty plant, so make sure to supply your plant with ample amounts of clean water.

Once your cannabis is through vegging, she will enter the flower stage. When this happens, you must set your timer to 12 hours on, and 12 hours off. This will produce a forest of luscious, pungent cannabis flowers.

One last thing to remember when growing indoors is spider mites. They will suffocate your plant by wrapping her leaves with their silky webs. A sure way to naturally get rid of these little pests, is to use neem oil. If you notice spider mites on your plant, act fast — as they are notorious for wiping out entire crops!

As we have explored both outdoor and indoor methods, you are now ready to choose your favored approach. Growing cannabis is a lot of work, and takes time, but once you get into a comfortable cycle, and can effortlessly produce gardens, the benefits will sustain you for a life time. Once you master the art of growing cannabis, you will never go without material for your extracts ever again!

Chapter 4:

How to Make Butane Hash Oil (BHO)

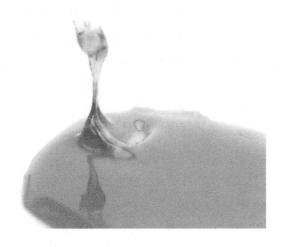

Honey Oil

BHO (Butane Hash Oil), known to many as "honey oil," is one of the oldest cannabis extracts around. This powerful oil has some CBD in it, but it is very, very high in THC, so be mindful when using. The

THC and CBD chemicals are pulled from the plant, leaving behind all the vegetation, and settling in a pure, aromatic oil. There are many ways to smoke BHO. However, the most traditional method is to apply it directly to a luscious, green bowl of cannabis.

If smoking BHO is your preferred method of use, then it is recommended that it is smoked for recreational purposes, as smoke can worsen certain health problems in the long run. Nonetheless, if you want to use BHO to treat medical issues, you can purchase vaporizers that will turn the oil into vapor, which is less taxing on the lungs.

In short, the process in which BHO is made proves to be simple: butane separates the cannabinoids from the plant matter and pushes it through a strainer. The instant result is a concoction of butane and cannabis goodness. Over time, the butane will evaporate by itself, but there are certain methods we can employ to speed this process up. It sounds simple enough, however there are supplies that you will need, and some safety precautions to keep in mind.

Safety and Such

When creating BHO on a smaller level, there are not too many safety precautions to be aware of. Make sure the materials are quality so they do not act defective, and that you are in an area that has good airflow (so butane does not build up).

It is also recommended to wear a mask to avoid the unwanted fumes. Also, you should wear safety glasses, just in case; it is always better to be safe than sorry. Now that we have covered the safety precautions, let us begin making some honey oil of our own!

Supplies Needed

- Cannabis
  The better cannabis flowers you use, the better quality your BHO will be. However, you can make this extract with leaves and clippings, which is a way people have been turning trash into gold for years.

- <u>Butane</u>

  As you may have guessed, since it can be found in the product's name (Butane Hash Oil), butane is a vital facet in this equation. It is recommended to use a 10 oz. can for every ounce of plant material.

- <u>Extraction Tube</u>

  It is necessary to use a glass extraction tube for this process. You can purchase these between $40 and $100, depending on size and manufacturer. It is highly recommended to get a durable extraction tube to avoid cracking glass.

- <u>Pyrex Dishes</u>

  You will need one medium and one large Pyrex dish. This heat resistant glassware will come in handy, and you can buy these almost anywhere.

- <u>Razor Blade Scraper</u>

  This item is easily accessible, and can be bought at any hardware store such as Ace or Home Depot.

- <u>Concentrate Container</u>
  These little containers will save you the trouble of wasting the precious cannabis oil, and they will store it to keep it fresh and potent. They are designed from a non-stick material, and can be bought at a smoke shop for around ten to fifteen dollars.

- <u>(Option 1) Electric Heating Pad</u>
  This household item can be found at any drug store. If you choose this, you won't be needing the following item.

- <u>(Option 2) Vacuum Purging System</u>
  The purging system is a more expensive option. Nonetheless, it makes the production process more effective. If you chose to use a vacuum purge, then you will not need a heating pad.

Okay, now that we have covered all the materials you will need, let us begin making some butane hash oil!

The Process

Step 1: Get Everything Ready

The first thing you will need to do is fill up your **extraction tube** with **cannabis plant material**. It is important that the plant material you use is completely dry, and that it is densely packed to avoid air bubbles from forming.

If your extractor tube did not come with a filter screen, then you can fasten a mesh coffee filter in its place at the larger end of the tube. Once your cannabis is packed tight, and your screen is fastened to the bottom, you are ready to begin.

Step 2: Extract Cannabinoids

Grab your **medium Pyrex dish**, and place it on a sturdy surface. Hold the extraction tube above the dish with the screen side on the bottom. In the smaller hole on top of the extractor, insert the **butane** nozzle, and fill the tube with butane. Gold liquid will begin to drip through the screen and onto the medium Pyrex dish. Continue this process until the liquid is no longer gold. This means that all the cannabinoids have been depleted from the flowers or leaves.

Step 3: Evaporation

You should now have a medium Pyrex dish full of golden oil and butane. The next step is to separate the hazardous butane from the honey oil. There are two ways to do this: The old-fashioned way, and the newer way.

The former is less expensive than the latter, but the process takes longer to complete. In either route, you should make sure the area you are in is well ventilated, and wear any kind of air filtering mask to avoid harmful fumes.

No matter the method used, whether it be old-fashioned or the modern way, you must start the same. Fill the **large Pyrex dish** with hot water and place the medium dish into it. The heating of molecules will begin the evaporation process, and the butane will begin to flee from the oil.

The old-fashioned way: If you use a **heating pad**, place the pad under the large Pyrex dish, and set it on high to steadily keep the water at a hot temperature. The evaporation process should take no longer than 60-90 minutes.

The modern way: When using a **vacuum purge**, the process will go by considerably faster. Just place the vacuum purge over the two dishes and let it do its thing! You will have butane-free, delicious honey oil between 10-20 minutes!

Evaporation has been achieved when the oil is completely without murky appearance. To double-check, *carefully* light a flame next to fresh hash oil. If it ignites, then you should continue the evaporation process.

Step 4: Store It & Enjoy

Take your razor blade scraper, and make sure to scrape all remnants of oil in the dish. Immediately transfer it into a concentrate container, so your honey oil will stay fresh, scrumptious, and potent for a long time. Finally, it is time to enjoy!

Chapter 5:

How to Make Rick Simpson Oil (RSO)

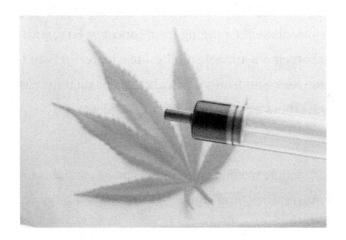

The Story of a Healer

Rick Simpson has been advocating and spreading knowledge about using medical cannabis to treat ailments, from minor to severe, for about ten years now. In 1997, Simpson began self-medicating himself with cannabis to aid a head injury that he suffered from. Rick Simpson's personal results from treating his head injury changed his life and, as time moved along, he began to spread his story of recovery — changing the lives of many along the way.

In 2003, Rick Simpson completely stifled skin cancer with the use of his cannabinoid oil recipe. This visionary began helping people who suffered from various ailments, ranging from cancer to HIV, with his homemade miracle oil. Besides the recipe, what made Rick Simpson's magical cannabis oil different from others was the method of *how to use* it.

Most people would traditionally smoke cannabis oils. However, Rick Simpson urged that this was ineffective if one is aiming to treat serious medical issues. Instead, Simpson urged people to apply the oil directly onto the skin, or to ingest it with food or beverages.

Not much time passed before RSO (Rick Simpson Oil) became widely accepted by the citizens of

Canada, as almost-miraculous stories of healing were emerging around the country.

Unfortunately, since cannabis was illegal in Canada, Rick Simpson's practice was eventually cut short by law officials. To the dismay of many, he was charged with an array of counts for trafficking marijuana, and many of the people who relied on his magical oil were stripped of their treatments.

Nonetheless, Rick Simpson passionately stood by his vision, and continued to spread the word. There was a new healer in the medical world, but a lot of people were not happy that it turned out to be cannabis.

The world has become a much different place since then, much thanks to the informational nature of the internet. Cannabis is no longer simply restricted to the description of "dangerous drug," as newer generations have brought with them open minds. Rick Simpson is one of the main reasons that so many have come to see cannabis in a different light.

His magical oil, consisting of cannabinoids purely extracted from the use of solvents (alcohol is the most common), has been a key factor in shaping the enlightenment pertaining to this helpful compound. RSO treks on, stronger than ever, into the new age, as this medical asset continues to sprout up miracles across the map. Are you ready to learn how to make your own healing oil?

Safety and Such

Before we begin, we would like to stress that this method of making cannabis extracts should be approached with caution, as the process is *extremely* flammable. Make sure to wear protective eyewear, as well as long sleeves and an air filtering mask.

Make sure the area you make your RSO in has good air flow, and have a nearby fan to aid with ventilation. DO NOT smoke around the production site, and stay away from any kind of stove tops and other heat sources that may spark a flame. Again, this process is very flammable. Safety first!

Now that you have all the necessary safety precautions in mind, let us make a list of what you will need to begin producing.

Supplies Needed

- Cannabis

  Try to have at least an ounce of cannabis. When making RSO at home, it is not recommended to exceed a pound of plant material. Also, make sure that it is extremely dry!

- Plastic Buckets

  Just plain old plastic buckets will do. The Home Depot buckets are good ones to use, as they are top quality. You will need two of them.

- Solvent

  You can use rubbing alcohol, butane, ethanol, or even water for a solvent. It is suggested to use 500 ml. for each ounce of plant material.

- A Crushing Stick

  Any kind of untreated wood will do. You can literally find a branch outside of your house, as long as it is durable enough.

- Rubber Gloves

  Heavy duty, multi-purpose rubber gloves will help you with this process.

- Strainer

  You can purchase a coffee mesh strainer for this. They are usually quite cheap.

- Crock Pot or Rice Cooker

  As this process is very flammable, using stove tops is strongly inadvisable, and is *extremely* unsafe. Reducing the solvent will heavily rely on either a crock pot or a rice cooker.

- Stainless Steel Container

  The size of this item will depend on how much oil you intend to produce.

- Coffee Warmer or Heating Pad

  This will be used for the final dehydration process

- (Recommended) A Plastic Syringe

  This is not mandatory, but it will help with

gathering and storing your RSO.

As you can see, the materials needed for manufacturing RSO yourself are quite basic, and obtaining them is not only easy, but inexpensive. Once you invest in these items, you will be able to make all the Rick Simpson Oil you so desire.

The Process

Step 1: An Easy Start

Simply take your **dry cannabis plant material** and put it in the bucket. In correspondence with the optimal ratio between **solvent** and plant material, as discussed in the supplies section, have your solvent measured out and ready.

Slowly pour the solvent onto the plant matter, but not all of it — just enough to dampen the plant material.

Step 2: Crush Time

Take your **wooden crushing stick**, the one that is not treated, and begin to crush up the dampened plant material. Do this until it is finely crushed, and then add more solvent; this time, soaking the plant material as you crush. Continue to crush and add more solvent when necessary (the plant material should be completely soaked).

This process should go on for about 3-5 minutes. Afterwards, you can pour the black oil into your other bucket. This rich black oil is almost pure THC (80+%)! Keep the plant material in the bucket and add more solvent; this is to gather the remaining (20% or so) THC in the plant. Continue to crush for another 3-5 minutes.

Dump the soaked plant material with the remaining 20% into the bucket with the 80% oil. Put on your heavy duty, **multi-purpose rubber gloves**, and discard of all the plant matter. Make sure to squeeze and squish the remains as much as you can with your hands, as this will give you more oil.

Step 3: Evaporation

Now you should have a bucket with pure THC oil, with remnants of plant material floating around. Grab your **stainless-steel container** and the **coffee filter**. Proceed to carefully pour the oil from the bucket through the filter and into the stainless steel container.

Transfer the oil from the container into your crock pot or rice cooker, as you will begin to slowly cook off the harmful solvents. Keep the stainless steel container nearby, as you will need it again.

Fill the **rice cooker or crock pot** up to about ¾ full of oil, and then turn up the heat to high. Remember, you must use a crockpot or rice cooker, as the solvents are highly flammable and should not be exposed to heavy levels of heat.

Over time, you will notice that the amount of liquid is reduced, as evaporation gradually removes the unwanted solvents. Continue to add your oil into the rice cooker or crock pot, until all of it is in the process of reduction. Once it reduces significantly, add about ten drops of water or so to the mixture — which helps separate the poisonous solvents from the oils. Keep at it until just a little bit of solvent water resides on top of the oil.

Once this happens, with oven mitts protecting your hands, pick up the cooker and swirl the solvent water around and around until you can see no more. Immediately turn the cooker down to low, as the oil should never reach over 290 degrees Fahrenheit. Then, get your stainless-steel container, and pour oil from the cooker into the stainless steel container.

Step 4: Wait, and Then Enjoy!

Once you have gotten your oil into the stainless-steel container, you must put the container on some sort of low heat to finish the evaporation process. This is where your **coffee warmer or your heating pad** come into play. Leave the stainless-steel container on the warming source until all liquid is gone and you are left with pure oil. This waiting game can take 3-4 hours, but patience will pay off; you want to be sure all solvents are long gone.

With your **plastic syringe**, suck up all the oil from the container, being diligent to get every drop (remember, each drop is pure THC, and thus valuable). The syringe will store the oil, keeping it fresh and effective, as well as acting as a great applier.

Now, all that's left to do is to enjoy! Remember, this is a potent oil, so be careful with your dosage. However, RSO is the most recognized form of cannabis extract for treating cancer, and it is highly recommended for medical use, as the oil works wonders on various severe ailments.

There are a lot of people out there who simply *pretend* to make this stuff. So, if you want some, it is wise to make it yourself. Well, now you can! Rick Simpson's vision lives on with you.

Chapter 6:

How to Make Tinctures

The Waiting Extract

Tinctures are remarkably simple in explanation, as well as in creation. Basically, tinctures are pure, liquid cannabis extracts, where alcohol is used to strip the cannabis of its THC. This powerful and efficient way to medicate is highly recommended for chronic pain, and thus, medical use. The pure THC liquid is known to offer the effects of cannabis to the user within fifteen minutes after applying but a few drops under the tongue; this stuff is very potent!

By far, this method of extract is the easiest out of them all, as all one must do is mix and wait. There are really no safety precautions to follow when making tincture, except to be careful to not use too much of the finished product. Are you ready to learn an effortless cannabis extract method? Well, all you must do is gather the materials, and then wait for chemistry to do its thing. It is really that simple.

Supplies Needed

- Cannabis
  You can use leaves, trimmings, or buds to make tinctures. Like all cannabis extracts, the better quality of plant material will result in a better cannabis extract.

- Pure Grain Alcohol
  You can buy this almost pure alcohol, known as Everclear, at most liquor stores. It is essentially used to make various types of different alcohol, and should *never* be consumed, as it is usually 90% or more alcohol. As you might expect, this stuff is highly flammable!

- Glass Jar
  Any glass jar will do, but it must have an air-tight seal (mason jars, for example). The size of the jar will depend on how much tincture you plan to make.

- Small Funnel and Strainer
  These will be essential to transporting your tincture. Just a traditional funnel and a coffee mesh filter will work.

- Medicine Bottle & Eyedropper
  This is used for storage and application purposes.

In all actuality, making cannabis tincture requires very little. You can get a bottle of Everclear for less than ten dollars. Mason jars, small funnels, strainers, medicine jars, and eyedroppers can be obtained with ease. To make this cannabis extract, the hardest thing to acquire is the plant material itself.

The Process

Step 1: Plan Accordingly

Firstly, you must have in mind approximately how much tincture you plan on making. Most extracts require a large amount of **cannabis** plant extract, but not this one. Minimum batches can be as small as 35 ml (or 1 ounce), with a ratio of 1 gram of plant material. However, the sky is the limit, and based on this ratio (1 gram to every 1 ounce of pure grain alcohol), you can make as much tincture as you please.

Step 2: Make the Concoction

This is the bulk of the work right here. Take your cannabis plant material, place it into the **mason jar** (one that is appropriately sized for the batch of course) and fill the jar with the designated amount of **pure grain alcohol**.

Keep in mind that each dose for this recipe is about 3-4 drops. 1 ounce of liquid produces roughly 24 drops, so if you made one gram of plant material to 1 ounce of pure grain alcohol, you will get around 6 doses. After you have mixed the plant material and the grain alcohol together, place it aside somewhere safe. It will now need to sit.

Step 3: Wait & Shake

For the next 5-10 days, make sure to revisit your tincture and shake it thoroughly. There is no set amount of time, but this is a good time limit for first time users. Some veteran users will soak their cannabis for weeks, or even months, producing a *very* powerful tincture. Remember, the longer you let it soak, the stronger it will become. Be diligent, and shake your tincture at least once a day.

Step 4: Store & Enjoy

Well, now that it has been a minimum of 5-10 days, chances are your tincture is ready for use. However, make sure to taste it first to try and test the strength; you may want a stronger batch. If this is the case, simply put the lid back on and let the jar sit longer.

If the tincture is ready and suitable to your needs, take your **little funnel and strainer**, and carefully transfer the liquid medicine into a medicine bottle. When you want to use this powerful tincture, take your **eyedropper**, fill, and enjoy!

Chapter 7:

How to Make Cannabutter

Cannabis Meets Culinary

This next cannabis product is one that has been
around for a long time. Knowing how to make this
really opens the door to a whole new world of
cannabis extracts.

Cannabutter presents almost a limitless array of methods of use, from spreading it onto a piece of toast, to dropping it into your coffee (perhaps unbelievably, this is very delicious). More remarkably, cannabutter is the sole base, and key builder, to the wonderful world of edibles (more on that in a bit).

Cannabutter is exactly how it sounds: cannabis + butter. The process when making it, in simple explanation, basically heats up the THC in the cannabis, and infuses it into the butter. The heating part is especially crucial, as simply eating cannabis raw is not efficient; the amount you would have to eat to have any noticeable effect would greatly upset your stomach, and will likely not do anything but that.

However, when you appropriately heat up cannabis, it activates the THC with a process called decarboxylation — basically heating up the dormant THCA (a THC precursor), and transforming it into THC. Smoking cannabis is essentially decarboxylation. When making cannabutter, you are draining the cannabinoids from the plant material, activating their THC molecules, and infusing them with the butter — a solvent that freezes the THC, leaving it activated within its grasp.

Safety and Such

Making this cannabis extract is very easy, and all the materials needed can usually be found in your home. If not, they can be acquired with little effort, as they are traditional cooking utensils. This process involves heat, so some safety precautions should be considered. They are, however, self-explanatory, and mirror precautions pertaining to normal cooking.

Wear long sleeves, keep a diligent eye on the boiling pot to make sure you do not burn anything, keep flammable things away from the cooking surface; you know, just the basics to know when cooking. With even the slightest experience in a kitchen, you will be ready to make this cannabis extract. So, are you ready? Let us start with what you will need.

Supplies Needed

- Butter

  This is essential to making cannabutter, and asks for a **1 cup butter** to ½ ounce cannabis ratio.

- Cannabis

  Cannabutter is great because you can make it with your leaves, as taste will be hidden in whatever you eat cannabutter *with*, or cook cannabutter *in*.

- Water

  Add **2 cups** of water to the 1 cup butter to ½ ounce cannabis ratio. For example, if you have 2 ounces of cannabis you wish to use for cannabutter, you will use 4 cups of butter, and 8 cups of water.

- Metal Strainer

  You can also use a cheesecloth, but you are more likely to own a metal strainer over a cheesecloth. This tool will be used to strain cannabis from the butter.

- Medium Sized Pan

  This is what you will cook your cannabutter

in. Keep a diligent eye on your cooking butter, as burning it will not just ruin your cannabutter, but also your pan!

- Bowl
  A glass bowl, at room temperature is suggested, but any bowl will do.

Crazy, huh? That is all you need. It would not be surprising to find (besides maybe the cannabis) all of this in your very own kitchen. So, what do you say? Grab those cannabis leaves that you planned to throwaway and head to your kitchen. Let's cook some cannabutter!

The Process

Step 1: Getting Started.

First, make sure to get all your measurements up to par with the **2 cups of water to 1 cup of butter to ½ ounce of cannabis** ratio. Once you have this all sorted out, grab your **medium sized pan**, and add water with the butter into it, while maintaining a medium heat level. The water needs to separate the butter from the pan, so if you think you need more, add more water.

Step 2: Cook the Cannabis.

Once you have your butter and your water nicely simmering, add your cannabis and turn the heat down to low. Mix thoroughly. Allow the simmering pot to go for 2-3 hours, making sure that you are keeping an eye on it and stirring it, so there will be no burning. It is wise to stir every 5-10 minutes.

Step 3: Strain It.

Now that you have simmered your cannabis for 2-3 hours, always remembering to make sure there is water in the pan (if the water begins to evaporate during previous step, make sure to add more of it accordingly), you are ready to strain it. First, give it a few minutes to cool down. Then, with your bowl ready, carefully pour your cannabis/water/butter concoction through the metal strainer and into the bowl. Now you will have a mixture of water and green, oily butter.

Step 4: Throw in the Fridge, Wait, Enjoy!

You are basically done. Throw the bowl in the refrigerator, and let the cannabinoid concoction sit over-night. In the morning, a green block of butter floating on the water like moss will greet you. Remove it, dry it off, and place in an air tight container for storage. You can keep your cannabutter in the refrigerator for weeks before it will spoil, but if you put it into the freezer, it will stay good for months!

Cannabutter can be applied onto a piece of toast, but it may be a little bitter in taste. However, dropping some in coffee works really well. Nonetheless, as mentioned, cannabutter's biggest attribute is the role that it plays in the culinary cannabis world, also known simply as "edibles".

Bonus Tip:

If you would rather make canna-oil, follow the same recipe, but instead of using butter, use vegetable oil. It makes for a healthier alternative. However, most people probably prefer the fuller taste of cannabutter.

Chapter 8:

How to Make Edibles,

Part I: Brownies & Cookies

Now that you have your cannabutter in your refrigerator, we can explore the world of edibles. This form of cannabis extract is by far the most delicious one, as the sky is the limit for cannabinoid-infused foods. Simply put, edibles are THC-infused items that you can eat. We will cover the most common and beginner-friendly edibles in this chapter. The basic edibles we will explore in this chapter are ones that you most certainly have heard of: pot brownies and weed cookies. These are the easiest edibles to make, and are highly recommended for newbies.

Pot Brownies

Pot brownies are the most famous of edibles, making their way into movies, TV shows, and the general knowledge of many. These appetizing cannabis treats are great for occasional recreational use, and is a good way to get an infusion of THC without any smoke.

Supplies Needed

- Cannabutter or Canna-oil
  To make canna-oil, refer to chapter 7 and follow the same recipe, but instead of butter, use vegetable oil. You will need **1 cup** of cannabutter, or canna-oil, for your brownies.

- A Baking Pan

  This item most likely already exists in your kitchen.

- A Small Stove Top Pan

  You can use the same pan that you used in *Chapter 7: How to make Cannabutter*.

- Brownie Mix

  Any brownie mix you desire.

- A Wooden Spoon

  This will be used to mix your brownie mix.

- Eggs

  You may use **two** eggs, but it all depends on the brownie mix of your choice.

The Process

Step 1: Melt the Cannabutter

In your **small/medium stove pan**, lightly heat up your **cannabutter** so it turns back into an oil. Do not over heat, or you will burn your cannabutter. If you are using **canna-oil**, then you will not need to worry about this step, as you will already have an oil based cannabis extract.

Once your cannabutter is melted, turn the stove to warm, and draw your attention to the brownie mix.

Step 2: Make the Brownie Mix

Proceed to mix your **brownie mix** with the **wooden spoon**. Brownie mixes usually call for the use of up to **two eggs**. Then, add your cannabutter or canna-oil to the **baking pan**. Once the green oil has settled on the floor of the pan, dump your brownie mix directly on top the cannabutter in your pan.

Step 3: Bake and Enjoy

Now that you have a baking pan full of cannabutter and brownie mix, throw it in the oven, preheated to 350 degrees, and set your timer for 30 minutes.

Check your brownies roughly every ten minutes to make sure they are good.

30 minutes may not be long enough, as sometimes it is known to take an hour. A good way to tell is when the top of the brownies become lightly crispy. Once ready, remove the scrumptious treats, let cool, and enjoy. Be careful in the beginning, as you should cautiously test their potency at first.

Weed Cookies

We will now teach you how to make the other basic, and popular, edible: the weed cookie. Just like pot brownies, these are great for occasional recreational use, but should probably not be consumed on a regular basis, like most cookies. You can make any cookie you like with cannabutter, from sugar cookies to macadamia cookies.

What makes cookies different, is that you can make them with dried cannabis plant material, as you are not limited to cannabutter or canna-oil. We will separate this section into two recipes, a classic chocolate chip cookie with dried cannabis plant material, and a white chocolate chip macadamia cookie with cannabutter. Yes, they really are as delicious as they sound!

The Classic Chocolate Chip Cookie with Dried Cannabis

Supplies Needed

- Cannabis
  You will need **¼ ounce** to **¾ ounce** of buds or trimmings, depending on your tolerance.

- Kitchen Utensils
  You will need **two medium sized bowls**, a **hand or electric mixer**, a **measuring cup**, a basic **measuring set**, a **wooden spatula**, or a **wooden spoon**, a **baking sheet**, and **baking paper**.

- Flour

  You will need **2 cups**.

- Baking Soda

  ½ teaspoon is what the recipe calls for.

- Salt

  Again, you will need **½ teaspoon** of this.

- Unsalted Butter

  ¾ of a cup will do.

- Brown Sugar

  1 cup, lightly packed is called for.

- White Sugar

  1/3 cup of white sugar is asked of.

- Vanilla Extract

  1 tablespoon will be needed.

- Eggs

  You will need **two eggs**, and one egg should be used just for the yolk.

- Chocolate Bar

  This should be broken up into small pieces and must amount to **1 cup**.

- Grinder

A coffee grinder will do.

The Process

Step 1: Start the Mix:

Begin by greasing up your **baking pan**, and preheating your oven to 350 degrees. Then, grab your **dried cannabis** and **coffee bean grinder**, and grind your plant matter to near dust. Add this fine cannabis dust to the other dry ingredients (**flour, baking soda and salt**) and put it aside.

Melt your **unsalted butter**, either by microwave or stove top, and add this with **white sugar** and **brown sugar**.

Mix thoroughly, beat in your **eggs** and **vanilla extract** and lastly, add your **broken-up chocolate bar.**

Step 2: Drop Those Cookies:

Drop your cookies onto your pre-greased pan. This recipe should yield 12-18 small cookies, or 10-12 medium-sized ones. Slide your cookies in the oven, and bake them for **15-20 minutes**; checking them often to make sure they are not overdone.

Step 3: Don't Burn Your Mouth:

The delectable cookies will be immediately screaming at you to eat them the very moment you take them out of the oven. However, be patient, and let them cool a bit before you dive in. Give them at least 5-10 minutes to cool, then enjoy!

Scrumptious White Chocolate Chip Macadamia Cookie with Cannabutter

Supplies Needed

- Cannabutter

  You will need **¾ of a cup** of cannabutter.

- Kitchen Utensils

  You will need **two medium sized bowls**, a **hand or electric mixer**, a **measuring cup**, a **basic measuring set**, a **wooden spatula**, or a **wooden spoon**, a **baking sheet**, and **baking paper**.

- Flour

  You will need **2 ¼ cups.**

- Baking Soda

  ½ teaspoon is what the recipe calls for.

- Salt

  You will need **½ teaspoon** of this.

- Brown Sugar

  1 cup, lightly packed is called for.

- White Sugar

  1/3 cup of white sugar is asked of.

- Vanilla Extract

  1 tablespoon will be needed.

- Eggs

  You will need **two eggs**, **one full egg** and **one egg should be used just for the yolk**.

- White Chocolate Chips

  1 cup of white chocolate chips is necessary; however, you can add more or use less if you prefer.

- Macadamia Nuts

  You will need **½ cup** of macadamia nuts broken into smaller pieces.

The Process

This process is very similar to making cookies with dried cannabis, however, do not be fooled by the similarities, as there are a number of slight differences that must be taken into account.

Step 1: Start the Mix:

Start the same as before, in the previous recipe, and grease up your pan after preheating your oven to 350 degrees. Mix your dry ingredients (**flour, baking soda and salt**) and place aside. Melt your **cannabutter** carefully on a stove top.

Once your cannabutter has successfully melted (heat up on low), add this with **white sugar, brown sugar**, and the rest of the dry ingredients.

Mix thoroughly, and then beat in your **eggs** and **vanilla extract**. Lastly, add your **white chocolate chips** and your broken-up **macadamia nuts**.

Step 2: Drop Those Cookies:

This recipe will make about 12-18 small cookies, or 10-12 medium-sized ones, just as the previous recipe. Slide your cookies in the oven, and bake them for **15-20 minutes**. Check them often, and allow to cook a little longer if you want crispy cookies (20-25 minutes).

Step 3: Don't Burn Your Mouth:

These delicious cookies will *also* be urging you to eat them the moment you take them out of the oven. Be patient and let them cool a bit before you dive in. Give them at least **5-10 minutes** to cool, then enjoy!

In this chapter, we learned how to make the most basic, and perhaps the most famous, of edibles: the pot brownie and the weed cookie.

However, with cannabutter, the culinary options vary widely, and we will continue to explore the "cannabinoid meets culinary arts" story in the next chapter, as we will go into more complicated dishes.

In the next chapter, we will teach you how to use edibles to make breakfast, lunch, dinner, *and* dessert!

Chapter 9:

How to Make Edibles,

Part II: Further Exploration

In the last chapter, we merely touched base on the wondrous world of edibles; brownies and cookies are not even the beginning! In this chapter, we will enter further exploration of the cannabis culinary world, as we will provide a full day's worth of meals: breakfast, lunch, dinner and desert.

Using cannabutter and canna-oils open an array of possibilities for culinary delights, so covering all the edibles would be to enter a never-ending book.

We will not be able to cover every recipe here, but our goal is to get you familiar with cooking with cannabutter or canna-oil. Once you can do that, then the list of potential edibles is virtually endless.

A good start for any day relies heavily on a hearty breakfast, and we are going to teach you how to make a delicious breakfast dish: the Belgian Waffle.

"Good Morning!" — The Cannabis Belgian Waffle

Supplies Needed

- <u>Waffle Iron</u>

  This kitchen utensil is essential to making your waffles easily and properly.

- <u>Cannabutter</u>

  Use about ½ **cup**.

- <u>Two Bowls</u>

  You will need **1 small** bowl and **1 medium** bowl.

- <u>Classic Egg Beater</u>

  You can do this by hand, or if you have a machine, well, that makes things even easier.

- <u>Wooden Spoon</u>

  For mixing.

- <u>A Small Stove Top Pan</u>

  This will make things easier.

- <u>Eggs</u>

  2 eggs will suffice, and you will be separating

the yolks from the whites.

- <u>Milk</u>

  2 cups, make sure the milk is warmed before using it.

- <u>White Sugar</u>

  5 tablespoons.

- <u>Vanilla Extract</u>

  1 ½ teaspoon.

- <u>Flour</u>

  2 ¾ cups.

- <u>Salt</u>

  A **teaspoon** or a **healthy pinch** will do.

- <u>(Optional) Maple syrup</u>

  To make this an even more enjoyable experience, it is wise to have pure maple syrup to add as you like. It is not required, however.

The Process

Step 1: Make the Mix

Firstly, grab your **small pan**, turn your stove top burner on low heat, and place **cannabutter** inside pan. In about ten minutes or so, you will have melted cannabutter. This will make your life easier when you are mixing. Next, get your **eggs** ready by separating the yolks from the whites; both parts will be used in this recipe.

Use your **wooden spoon** to mix the **warm milk, flour, sugar,** cannabutter, **egg yolks, vanilla extract**, and **salt** together thoroughly in the **medium sized bowl**. Be sure that your batter is consistent.

Now take your **egg whites**, and use your **egg beater** to beat them in the **smaller bowl**. Do this for at least 3-5 minutes, then add this to your ingredients in the medium bowl. Let sit for roughly 40 minutes.

Get your **waffle iron** ready, with some oil and sufficient heat. Pour your mixture into the waffle iron, and cook until golden browning begins. Let your waffles cool, and there you go! Now, relax and, if you wish, drizzle some pure maple syrup on your cannabis-infused Belgian waffles, and get your day started on a high note!

"Good Afternoon!" — Homemade Cannabis Macaroni and Cheese

Supplies Needed

- Cannabutter
  Use **½ cup** of your cannabutter.

- Cheese
  You will need **½ cup of shredded cheddar**, and **½ cup of shredded mozzarella** cheese.

- Medium Sized Pan

This is crucial.

- Water

  6 cups will be sufficient.

- Pasta

  For this recipe, use small-sized pasta shells. **1 normal-sized box** will do.

- Black Pepper

  1 tablespoon.

- Pasta Strainer

  A medium or large sized pasta strainer will work for this dish.

- Heavy Whipping Cream

  ½ cup.

This dish is great for a satisfying lunch, and can either be a small side dish or the main course, as this cheesy deliciousness is just *that* hearty. If you wish, you can add bacon as well; cook two pieces of bacon, mince, and add to the final dish.

The Process

Step 1: Getting Started.

Take your **medium sized pan**, and bring water to a boil. Add your **pasta**, and turn down to ¾ of full heat. Cook for 8-10 minutes. Once this is done, pour your pasta into the **strainer**, and rinse with hot water from your sink. Allow pasta to drain for no more than 2 minutes.

Step 2: Put It All Together.

Now, grab your **cannabutter**, and add to the empty pan. Put heat on low to properly melt the cannabutter. Once it is melted, add your pasta, and stir thoroughly. Add your **cheese, cream,** and **black pepper**. Stir fervently for 3-5 minutes.

Step 3: Let Cool & Enjoy

Allow your mac & cheese to cool for 5 minutes, then enjoy. This is a great side dish for any lunch. Add bacon to make your mac & cheese to make it the main dish: two pieces cooked of cooked bacon, minced, and added to the final stirring process.

"Good Evening!" — Red Mashed Potatoes with Cannabis

Supplies Needed

- Cannabutter

  ½ cup to **¾ cup**, depending on your preference.

- Garlic

  You will need **2-3 cloves**.

- Salt

  1 tablespoon.

- Pepper

  1 tablespoon.

- Red Potatoes

  These are usually quite small, so **10-12** is recommended.

- Large Pan

  This will be your main tool.

- Wooden Spoon

  For stirring purposes.

- Heavy Whipping Cream

  ½ cup.

- Strainer

  A traditional pasta strainer will do.

The Process

Step 1: Boil the Taters

With your **large pan**, bring water to a boil. Rinse and cut your **red potatoes** into fourths (do not peel), and carefully add them to the boiling water. Turn the heat down to ¾ intensity — between medium and high.

While stirring occasionally, cook potatoes from 10-15 minutes, or when a fork easily pierces into them. While waiting, finely mince your **garlic**. Dump the potatoes into the **strainer**, and place the large pan back onto stove top; turning the heat down to 1/4, between low and medium.

Step 2: Mash It Up

First, add your **cannabutter**, and allow most of it to melt. Then, add your minced garlic and stir into the cannabutter, do this for about 3 minutes. Now, grab your steaming red potatoes, and add them to the pot.

Start mashing with the wooden spoon — stirring while you do so. Add the **heavy whipping cream** and continue stirring, gradually adding **salt** and **pepper**. Keep stirring until the potatoes are clearly mashed, and have a gentle fluffiness about them.

Step 3: Cool & Enjoy

Let your cannabis-infused mashed potatoes cool for 5-8 minutes, as this will allow them to reduce the remaining flavors into the taste. Serve as a side dish for any fitting dinner!

"Goodnight!" — Cannabis Toffee Crumble for Ice Cream Desert

Supplies Needed

- Cannabutter
  Use **¾ of a cup** for this recipe.

- Candy Thermometer
  You can buy one of these at Walmart, or you can order it on Amazon. They are cheap — around $10-$15.

- Salt
  Just a **pinch.**

- Sugar
  1 cup.

- <u>Vanilla Extract</u>
  1 teaspoon.

- <u>Chocolate Chips</u>
  Have **1 cup** of these ready.

- <u>Chopped Walnuts</u>
  ½ cup.

- <u>Medium Sauce Pan</u>
  This will be your main tool.

- <u>Baking Pan</u>
  A cookie sheet will do.

- <u>Wooden Spoon</u>
  For stirring.

- <u>Ice Water</u>
  Merely **2 tablespoons** will do.

<u>The Process</u>

<u>Step 1: Make the Candy.</u>

First, grease up your **cookie sheet** and set it aside.
Next, grab your **medium sauce pan**, and put it over

medium heat on a stove top. Mix **sugar, cannabutter**, and **1 tablespoon of ice water**, save the other tablespoon for later.

Cook on medium for 12-15 minutes while maintaining a diligent watch, as well as stirring the liquid candy with your **wooden spoon** often. When the **candy thermometer** reads 300 degrees, your candy is ready.

Step 2: Dump, Crack, and Enjoy.

Dump your scalding candy mix onto the greased-up cookie sheet. Once your candy is all on the cookie sheet, you will notice that it is quickly solidifying. The moment it is hardened, add the remaining **tablespoon of ice water** on it; spreading the water around the surface of the hard candy.

This will crack the toffee. Carefully, top some vanilla bean ice cream with the warm cannabis toffee, and finish the day off right!

These methods are more recommended for occasional recreational use, as snacking on butters and sugars can be unhealthy in the long run. However, if your health agrees, they are great, tasty alternatives for medicating with cannabis.

With the basic knowledge above, what did we learn? We learned that cooking with cannabutter is largely the same as cooking with regular butter. Find yourself some more recipes that require butter or oil, and these are usually perfect for making cannabis edibles.

Chapter 10:

How to Make Hash

History of Hashish

The story of hashish goes deep into history, clearly making it one of the oldest cannabis extracts around. Hashish dates to around 900 A.D. in Arabia, but some legends iterate that hash has been around for maybe thousands of years more. Around 1200 AD, a tale of assassins using this early cannabis extract made its way to Europe, and soon after, early scientists began exploring its medical qualities. The end of the nineteenth century marked the time when pharmaceutical companies started controlling the market. This was when cannabis was outcast as an outlaw.

Now, in the 21st Century, the recognition that cannabis lost so long ago has been regathered, and its presence in the medical world is becoming strong once again. Even for recreational purposes, it has become one of the most preferred methods of relaxation. Hash is one of the easiest extracts to make, and there are literally hundreds of different approaches one can take when gathering the "golden dust".

The methods to obtain hash have changed over the years, but hash itself has remained the same. Hash is THC separated from the plant, as the trichomes, or little white hairs, are stripped of their THC crystals — producing a pure and effective way to medicate, or simply a great option to just kick back and relax. In this chapter, we will cover some of the most basic methods to make hash, as they are the easiest and fastest ways. Are you ready to carry this ancient cannabis tradition into the future?

Harvest Hash

Known also as "Finger Hash", this is about as easy as it gets when it comes to making hash. However, this extract method does come with a catch, as it depends heavily on the harvest. When harvesting a plant, one will go through the trimming process, which happens right after the plant is pulled, or after it completely dries.

The point of this is to clean up the buds, to remove leafy vegetation from the precious buds. While you are going through this tedious process, you will notice an instant reward; a golden-brown gunk will begin to accrue on your clippers and fingers.

Remove this sticky substance from the clipper blades

with a paper clip, and roll the stickiness off your fingers. This will begin to form in a little ball. Guess what? You just made hash! You can pack this pure hash over a nice bowl of green flowers for recreational purposes, or you can vaporize it for a great medical alternative. This hashish almost makes *itself*, as long as you find a good harvest.

Blend Up Some Hash

For this method, all you will need is **dried cannabis, a blender, two glass jars, a silk screen,** and a **coffee mesh strainer**. Also, have some **ice cubes** available.

There is no danger involved, thus no specific safety precautions. Blending up some hash is another fast and easy method to make hashish. Here is how you do it!

The Process

Step 1: Blend It.

Add you **dried plant material** (the more the material, the more hash, so there really is no set amount) to your **blender,** along with the **ice cubes**. Add water (a sufficient amount to soak the plant material) and push the blend button. Continue the blending for about 1 minute or so to break down the fiber.

Step 2: Strain & Settle It.

Now that you have a cannabis smoothie, pour the vibrant green liquid through the **silk screen**, and into one of the **glass jars**. Give your green liquid 20-30 minutes to settle.

Step 3: Final Settle & Enjoy.

You will now notice the hash settling at the bottom of the jar. Remove about 2/3 of the surfacing water, and then add more. This will further settle your hash.

Carefully remove water from the settled hash by dumping the majority out, then strain the rest of it through the **coffee mesh filter**, and into your other **jar**. You now have some delicious hashish!

The Classic Screen Hash

This method is probably the most popular method. All you need is some **cannabis** flowers or trimmings, a **small mesh screen**, a **credit card**, and a **mirror** of some kind (relatively large, as this will be used to catch the trichomes).

Again, there are no safety precautions to heed to when doing this. This method does not prove to be as effective as the others in producing great hash, but it *is* the cheapest and most convenient.

The Process

Step 1: Getting Started.

Place your **small mesh screen** on top of the glass **mirror**. Then, add your **cannabis** to the screen.

Step 2: Slide Your Card, & Enjoy

Slide your **credit card** back and forth on the screen, essentially pushing the flowers, or trimmings, around on the screen. The THC from the trichomes will begin to scrape off as you gently proceed with this action. In no time at all, your glass will be covered in hash. However, there will still be a significant amount of THC in those flowers or trimmings, so do not throw them away. These will be perfect for making cannabutter, as we covered in previous chapters.

In this chapter, we lightly touched on some very popular methods to produce hash. Nonetheless, there are many other, more advanced methods and forms of hash. In the next chapter, we will explore one of the most popular of these: bubble hash.

Chapter 11:

How to Make Bubble Hash

Bubble Hash gets its name from the "bubble bag" it is produced in. Like plain old hash, bubble hash is a pure form of the cannabinoids stripped from the trichomes. The method itself makes bubble hash different in appearance, and when you smoke this cannabis extract it is known to bubble — another quality contributing to its name. While regular hash is usually a golden brown, bubble hash can be either pitch black, a luscious green, a soft yellow or the traditional golden brown. Bubble hash also comes in different textures, depending on the strain of cannabis.

Bubble hash can be enjoyed in many ways, from enjoying it in a water pipe, or adding it to joints. Again, it can be used recreationally or medically, but it depends on your medical condition. Some medical conditions allow for vapors, but it is usually safe to say that avoiding smoke when preexisting health conditions exist is wise.

Bubble Hash is one of the most natural methods to make hash, as the solvent used is simply ice water. Besides having the specialized bubble bag kit, everything else you will need to make this cannabis extract is found in most kitchens.

This cannabis extract method is also extremely safe, and calls for no special precautions to be taken. So, are you ready to make some bubble hash? Let us begin with materials.

Supplies Needed

- Cannabis

  Flowers or trimmings will suffice, however, trimmings are recommended, as this method turns that trash into gold. Your cannabis material *must* be frozen. For this recipe, you will need 4 small, traditional sandwich bags full of frozen cannabis — or about **4 ounces**.

- Bubble Bag Kit

  The most basic kit is that of 5 bags: a main, working bag, and 4 micron bags that start at 23 microns in size and get larger. Each bag will produce a different kind of bubble hash.

- Mixer

  You can either use a **wooden spoon** if you are planning to mix by hand, or a traditional **egg beater**. One of the best mixers for this recipe, but one that is not very common, is a **mixing drill** used for construction when mixing mortar and cement. If you have one of these, this will be the best tool to use. Make sure it's perfectly clean, though!

- Buckets
  Just **2**, plain old, **5 gallon** buckets. The durable, orange Home Depot buckets work very well for making bubble hash.

- Spoon
  Just a regular table spoon.

- Ice and Water
  2 small bags of ice will work, and make sure that the water you are using is cold and, preferably, filtered.

This method of making hash takes a little bit of time, but the rewards reaped are bountiful and well worth the while.

The Process

Step 1: Get Set Up.

A strong base for any project is a strong set up. Have your **ice and water** at hand. Have your **2 buckets** in front of you as well. In one bucket, add some ice — about 3 healthy scoops. Place your main "working" **bubble bag** inside this bucket, add more ice, before adding your frozen, dried **cannabis plant material**. Top with more ice and add water until all plant material is submerged and soaked.

Step 2: Mix and Mash.

Now you will have 1 bucket with your main bag, filled with cannabis, water, and ice. The other bucket should be empty (we will use that in just a moment). Take your **mixer** (whether it be an egg beater, wooden spoon, or mixing drill) and mix plant material in ice water thoroughly for 10-15 minutes. After some strong mixing and smashing, allow it to settle for 10-20 minutes.

Step 3: Get Your Bags Ready.

You will now have a bucket full of ice water, and cannabis. It is time to get your other bucket ready now. Prepare your **4 bubble bags**.

The smallest micron bag should go into the bucket first, then the next size up inside that one, then the next inside that one, and so forth. You will have four bags in your second bucket.

Step 4: Strain Main Bag.

Your first, main bag is ready to pull up. Slowly, while softly shaking the bag, pull the main bag up through the murky water. Make sure to strain all the water through the main bag.

All that should be left inside of the main bag is the plant material stripped of its cannabinoids, and the five-gallon bucket should be full of murky looking water. Pour this water into the other bucket with your 4 micron bags.

Step 5: Layers of Hash.

Take your first bag, and slowly shake it free from the other bags. After you pull this first bag up, you should notice that some hash has built up in the bottom of the filter.

Use your **spoon** and collect this gold, making sure to set aside this creamy substance onto a safe surface. Now, repeat the same process with the next bag, and then the next, and then with the next.

Each bag should yield more bubbly goodness at the bottom. With each yield, remove the hash and set it aside. After you have pulled up all your bags, the water solvent should be stripped of all the cannabinoids, and you should have a surface with four different piles of creamy bubble hash. Your work is done.

Step 6: Let Dry & Enjoy.

After giving your hash about **15-20 hours** to dry,

you will notice that the once creamy substance is now more of traditional looking hash. Each pile will be a different color depending on the strain you used to make your bubble hash. However, these little piles are ready for enjoyment.

Make sure to store each little pile separately, and apply to any joint or vaporizer; depending on how you choose to use your bubble hash. Now kick back, watch your hash bubble, and relax. After all the hard work, it is time to enjoy.

Chapter 12:

How to Make Kief

The Oldest Form of Hash

Kief is the earliest form of hash, and this cannabis extract goes by the name of "dry hash." Hash is usually clumpy, almost brown and sugar-like, or it is an oil, whereas kief is purely a green powder — a collection of the cannabinoids in its most basic form.

In other words, kief is hash in its simplest state.

Like most cannabis products, kief can be used medically or recreationally. Vaporizing this extract proves to be a great medical alternative, as opposed to smoking it. There are two methods to get kief, and one is so simple that we like to consider it the "kill-two birds-with-one-stone technique". However, before we get into making kief, the real magic behind kief is the various ways one can smoke it, so we will explore some of these traditional methods first.

Using Kief

One popular way to use kief is to sprinkle the green dust into a joint or onto a pipe load. Some like to smoke it pure with a screen through a water pipe to open up the flavors. Kief can be vaporized as well, by adding it to a vaporizer, or pouring it into a cartridge of e-cig liquid.

Another way kief can be used is to press it into hash.

To do this, simply grab some parchment paper and a hair straightener. Fill parchment paper with kief, fold, press with hair straightener (on medium heat) for 5 seconds, and there you go: hash. This method of making hash is nowhere near as efficient as methods mentioned earlier in this book. However, it is one of the simplest ways to use kief.

Kief has also found its way into the culinary world, as it is a main ingredient in cannabutter formulas, and it can be added to dry edible recipes to make them more potent, or to replace large amounts of unrefined plant material.

Now that you have some great methods in mind, let us explore two ways to make this ancient cannabis extract. One is very easy, and the kief will accumulate over time as you roll cannabis joints. The other takes more cannabis, and more effort. However, it produces *mountains* of kief. We will begin with the first method, which we like to call the "kill-two-birds-with-one-stone technique," also known as the grinder method.

Killing-Two-Birds-With-One-Stone Technique
A.k.a. The Grinder Method

Every time you roll a joint, or have broken up cannabis flowers with your fingers, you have met kief — that crystal-like, green powder on your fingertips. Nonetheless, collecting kief off your fingers when rolling a joint would prove quite ineffective.

Luckily for us, there is a tool that makes rolling joints easier *and* will collect kief for later use — thus, giving the name to the technique. All you will need is any cannabis of your choice, and a kief grinder with three chambers.

Every time you break up cannabis to roll a joint, or for any other reason, use your three-chamber kief grinder. In the top chamber, insert your unbroken cannabis flowers. Put the lid on and grind.

Next, you will unscrew your grinder to expose the second chamber. Here is where your chopped-up cannabis will be for rolling joints, or water pipe hits, or anything else; it really depends on what you chose to use the cannabis for.

Now, here is where the kief comes in. There is another chamber, the third and lowest one, and when you unscrew this one, you will notice a buildup of kief steadily collecting inside. For a steady smoker, one can accumulate up to a half gram of kief in a week — and all by just smoking cannabis!

Dry Ice Kief

This method is a little more complicated and makes a kief that is more suitable for culinary additions. You can drop this kief in soup or even add it to ice cream. In fact, you can add this dry iced kief to any dish you wish. Before we begin, lets gather some supplies.

Supplies Needed

- Cannabis

  You will need anywhere between **1 ounce** and **1 ½ ounce** of **dried cannabis** plant material.

- Baking Sheet

  A traditional baking sheet will do.

- Parchment Paper

  Also known as cookie sheet paper.

- Dry Ice

  A small bowl (**about 12 ounces**) of dried ice.

- Bubble Bag

  A **1 gallon bubble bag** with a **120-micron screen** will work fine.

- Heat Resistant Dish

  A **ramekin** used for custards or other baked goods will do.

- Scraper

  A **credit card** will suffice.

Now that we have all the supplies, let us begin

making our dry iced kief!

The Process

Step 1: Break Up the Cannabis.

It is stressed to do this by hand, as you will not lose a lot of kief this way. Break up all your **cannabis**, and add it to your **bubble bag**.

Step 2: Ice It & Sift It.

With the **parchment paper** laid inside of your **baking sheet**, hold your bubble bag full of cannabis above it. Add your **dry ice** to the bubble bag, and gently shake; to sift the kief onto the baking sheet and parchment paper.

Step 3: Collect It & Bake It.

Now, you will notice quite a bit of kief on your parchment paper. With your **scraper**, gather all your kief, and transport it into your **ramekin**. Preheat your oven to **250 degrees**, and bake your kief for no longer than **20 minutes**. Carefully remove your kief, and add to any dish of your liking!

After exploring some methods of gathering the most ancient cannabis extract out there, kief, we would like to follow this chapter with what the future has brought. As we find ourselves in the 21st century, discoveries and breakthroughs have met the world of cannabis, and the most recent one is called rosin; the cannabis innovation that brought about the dab culture.

Chapter 13:

How to Make Rosin

& "Do a Dab"

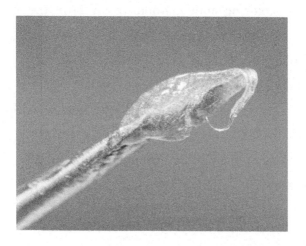

The Superhero Hashish

Although the prominent use of dabs has become increasingly popular in more recent times, the potent cannabis extract, known as rosin, has been on the menu since the 1960's. However, the current day dab, or more specifically, rosin, is far more potent than any older form of this derivative. Modern technology and instruments for making cannabis extracts has brought with them the innovation of non-solvent cannabinoid oils, hence this superhero hash: rosin.

The sometimes 90%+ THC extract has a story that matches that of a superhero, as this cannabis extract was the result of ten years' research in a laboratory, somewhere in British Columbia, Canada. Canadian scientists have had their eyes fixated on the magic that walks prominently next to cannabis, long before Americans.

Now that the cannabis wave has moved its way south to the States, more pure and clean forms of cannabinoids have been sought after. It was 2010 when rosin, more popularly known as the dab, found its way into the United States. Upon its arrival, through a laboratory in North America, it has been quickly asserting its fame — claiming a popularity currently unmatched by any other extract.

This high-powered, solvent-free hash oil, like all cannabis products, can be used for recreational or medical purposes; although, once again, if smoking disagrees with your health, this one is primarily suggested for recreational use. The intensity of the pure cannabis oil extract exceeds any formal BHO or Bubble Hash you have ever tried.

With this being said, it is highly recommended that only senior smokers use rosin, and one should especially take heed when taking a dab. If you do not heed to the strength and power of rosin, then you are potentially trekking in unpleasant waters. A too powerful dab, or rosin dose, will have you on the ground — quite literally!

Safety and Such

Although this superhero hash oil was first made in a laboratory, there is a method we will explore that makes producing rosin easier than you may have thought. Before attempting this, make sure to do this in an area with no carpet or flammable surroundings (such as a garage, for example).

Wear rubber gloves to protect your fingers from hot oil. This method of extract is completely solvent free, thus making it easy to make. However, to make a lot of this oil, it demands a lot of cannabis, and rosin is always made with the flower. After learning what comes next, you will then be ready to take a dab, but first let's make our rosin.

Supplies Needed

- A Hair Straightener
  Yes, that's right. This is actually what we will use to make our dabs.

- Parchment Paper
  Also known as cookie sheets — a non-stick paper for baking.

- Cannabis
  As mentioned, any dab should be made with the flower itself.

For having such a complex history in the laboratory, it is interesting to note how easy this cannabis extract oil is to make in your very own home!

The Process

Step 1: Getting Started.

Wrap your **cannabis flower** in the **parchment paper**, and heat up your **hair straightener** to medium heat.

Step 2: Press It.

With the flower encapsulated by the parchment paper, clamp tightly with the hair straightener. Press for 5 seconds, and repeat 2-3 times. You will notice a golden oil beginning to gather around the edges of the parchment paper.

Step 3: Wait, and Enjoy!

When you unfold your parchment paper, you will have a smashed cannabis flower, and yellow-golden oil surrounding it on the paper. Once cooled down, remove the smashed bud and enjoy your fresh rosin oil!

Just like traditional hashish, rosin can be added to a bowl of green, or can be vaporized; the latter is recommended when using for medical reasons. This new-age extract has also formulated its very own method for use: The dab.

Now that you have made your scrumptious rosin, we will now explain how to properly "take a dab"; for this is the most authentic and exciting route to take when stepping into the rosin experience.

Dabbing

Again, we will stress the power behind a dab, as even a dab the size of a sweat bead can prove extremely effective — so be careful and do not overdo it! To really take a ride on "dab mountain", you will only need a few things.

Supplies Needed

- **A Glass Oil Rig**

  This specialized piece of glassware, also known as a Dab Rig, can be purchased at any head shop, dispensary, or it can be ordered online. It is essentially a water pipe, but instead of a glass bowl, it has an attachment known as joint, in which you put a glass nail — which you heat up very hot and apply your dab upon. Another glass attachment, called the dome, is place around the nail when Dabbing.

- **A Large Butane Torch**

  This will need to be large enough to satisfy the size of the "nail" on your glass oil rig.

- <u>A Dabber</u>

  This is the tool that you use to apply your dab, or rosin, onto the glass nail with. They come in glass or metal, but cannabis enthusiasts usually prefer the metal ones. They look like little metal pens, but without the actual pen. You *could* just use a paper clip to apply your dab, but this is not recommended.

The two specialized items in the list above, the Glass Oil Rig and the Dabber, usually come together when you purchase a **Dab Rig Set**. Besides these three tools, you will need your **Rosin oil concentrate** of preference. OK! Let's get "Dabbed"!

<u>The Process</u>

<u>Step 1: Getting Started</u>

Fill your **glass oil rig** with water, and place the **glass nail** into the attachment of your rig — called **the joint**.

Take your **torch**, and heat your nail until it turns orange, keeping in mind to point the torch flame away from you, and your glass rig. Now, take your **dome attachment piece** and place it around the nail.

Allow the nail to slightly cool for 10-30 seconds, so as not to completely burn up your oil, and to achieve a full taste. If you wait too long, however, your nail will not burn the oil. This step will take a few tries to figure out when you get a brand new **dab Rig Set**.

Step 2: Separate

Grab your **dabber**, and separate just a small bead of r**osin oil**. Make sure to snag the oil by the edge, so the dab can easily fall off your dabber.

Step 3: Enjoy!

Begin to slowly suck air through your water pipe, and place the rosin on the hot nail. This will instantaneously vaporize, and you will swiftly have a mouth full of delicious cannabinoid smoke. Immediately remove your dome piece, so it is not subjected to getting stuck to your rig. Now, enjoy the experience!

This new way of usage has swept the cannabis world off its feet. With the exploration of rosin and the coming of the dab, cannabis users everywhere have found a new way to use little amounts of cannabis material to powerfully feel her wonders.

The early popularity of hashish faded with the nineteenth century, and it seemed that the age of cannabis extracts met its end. These two innovations, however, have now resurrected it, and have paved the way for science and cannabis to fully combine.

With the coming of rosin, and methods such as dabbing, it is exciting to see where the future is heading. As the age of cannabis extracts breathes again, it is thrilling to think that we are only at the beginning.

Chapter 14:

Looking Forward to

the Future

Cannabis extracts have come a long way. As we have explored in this book, they actually date back to ancient times, and once shined center stage in the medical field in certain cultures. The coming of the

20th century brought with it the humungous pharmaceutical drug companies, outlawing the healing cannabis plant altogether.

Now, cannabis is slowly but surely being welcomed back into the medical field, and society as a whole. The once-hated drug has become known as what it truly has always been: a healing plant. With its legalization in so many States during recent times, exploration of this medical wonder has finally been able to flourish, bringing about many wonderful innovations such as cannabis extracts for us to enjoy.

In this book, we took you on a journey into the cannabis extract kitchen, and explored wonders from ancient extracts, such as **Kief** and **Hash**, to more modern extracts, such as **Bubble Hash** and **Rosin**.

We smoked **BHO**, ate a four-course meal with **Cannabutter** and **Edibles**, and found time to relax with some potent **Tinctures**. In the end, our goal was to educate you, and teach you, how to make cannabis extracts. But why?

As science takes its time strolling through the cannabis garden, groundbreaking discoveries have popped up, and stories woven from miracles have emerged. Nature carries perfection somewhere in her bosom, we just have to seek sincerely, without judgement, in order to find it. That is why we have presented this book to you.

Cannabis seems to hold a key to ailments, mental and physical, and having the power to create this medicine is, well, something we think everyone should have. As minds start to bloom, cannabis has only just begun sharing her story.

Made in the USA
Middletown, DE
03 July 2019